KNIT KIMONO

KNIT KIMONO

18 DESIGNS with SIMPLE SHAPES

VICKI SQUARE

INTERWEAVE PRESS.
interweave.com

Design Susan Wasinger
Photostyling Susan Wasinger
Illustrations Vicki Square
Photography John Mueller
Technical Editing Karen Frisa

 Interweave Press LLC
201 East 4th Street
Loveland, CO 80537-5655 USA
interweave.com

Printed and bound in China by Asia Pacific.

Library of Congress Cataloging-in-Publication Data

Square, Vicki, 1954-
  Knit kimono : 18 designs with simple shapes / Vicki
Square, author.
      p. cm.
  Includes index.
  ISBN 978-1-931499-89-7 (pbk.)
  1. Knitting--Pattterns. 2. Kimonos. I. Title.
TT825.S71385 2007
746.43'2041--dc22

                              2007001891

10 9 8 7 6 5 4 3 2 1

ACKNOWLEDGMENTS

I count it a privilege to work at what I love. Without a question, however, a project of this magnitude is a big team effort, and I am so grateful to everyone at Interweave Press who has been a part of bringing this book to fruition. Thank you Linda Ligon, founder and original visionary of Interweave Press, for giving me opportunity and letting me offer my artistic vision to kimono. Thank you to Marilyn Murphy for believing in me, to Linda Stark for all her encouragement and marketing expertise, to Tricia Waddell for her professional direction, to Paulette Livers for her hand in the art direction. My heartfelt thanks go to Ann Budd for her expert editing and oversight, her constant encouragement, and her gentle way. Thank you to Karen Frisa for excellent technical editing. Thanks go to Susan Wasinger for artistic book design and photo styling and to photographer John Mueller.

To my knitting family, I love you all and I'm so grateful to have you support me so wholeheartedly, with your time, your exceptional skill, and your kind words and prayers. Lois Eynon, Joan Pickett, Micky Shafer, Sally Thieszen, Nancy Hewitt, Alice Bush, and Karen Tadich. This book would still be in the works without all of you.

To all the yarn companies who so graciously provided yarn to fulfill the vision I had for each kimono, I thank you: Berroco, Blue Sky Alpacas, Brown Sheep, Cascade, Classic Elite, Dale of Norway, Debbie Bliss, Fiesta, Louet, Mission Falls, Plymouth, Reynolds, Southwest Trading. What a joy to use so many exquisite yarns.

Thank you to my family, who are always there to cheer me on, my husband, Johnny, son, Alexander, daughter and husband, Justine and Jeffrey.

For Johnny, the love of my life

KNIT KIMONO

INTRODUCTION

I have always been enchanted by the beauty and timelessness of the Japanese kimono. From casual to formal, the kimono shape has transcended time and for centuries has been a fashion cornerstone for peasantry and nobility alike. The classic rectangular, yet streamlined and elegant shape is recognized worldwide as an icon of Japanese life and culture.

As a history buff, I'm fascinated by how the kimono has lasted through the ages, yet remains contemporary. The craftsmanship and precision in detail is a reflection of the structure of their society, of the beauty of organization, and of the simplicity of function.

As a knitter, I'm drawn to the simple shape and construction of kimono. The rectangular pieces give me the opportunity to enjoy the peaceful meditation of knitting row after row without having to pause to think about shaping. Even the finishing involves just a few straightforward seams. If you've only knitted scarves, you can knit a kimono—think of it as a few straight scarves sewn together.

As a clothing designer, I can't help but marvel how so many simple geometric elements combine to create a garment that looks great on every imaginable body type—from short to tall, narrow to wide, and everything in between. With the right combination of yarn, stitch pattern, and gauge, kimono offers beautiful drape and fluidity of movement that's always in style.

As an artist, I'm intrigued by the way that the simple shape can become a canvas for color, pattern, and design. From just a touch of color at the edgings to a stitch or color pattern that covers the entire garment to artistic splashes of embroidery, the possibilities for design are endless.

Each kimono in this collection represents my knitted interpretation of a style or feature of traditional kimono. The styles and shapes of the garments run the gamut from short to long, rectangular sleeves to shaped, straight or overlapping front opening, with sleeves or without, casual to dressy. I've selected yarns and stitch patterns that drape and move as beautifully as their woven counterparts. The versatility of the kimono is showcased in this collection, where you'll find entirely wearable wraps from tops to jackets to light coats, all with a contemporary flair. Whether you want to follow tradition or invent your own style, you can't go wrong with a kimono.

VICKI SQUARE

Kimono Basics

The Japanese kimono is a timeless garment that is based on the simplest construction involving nothing but rectangular pieces of cloth. From simple work clothes to elegant formal attire for nobility, the kimono runs the gamut from subdued and practical to flamboyant and ostentatious. Add to this versatility the fact that a kimono looks good on any body type—from huge sumo wrestler to petite geisha—and you've quite possibly got the ideal garment.

The kimono shape is certainly ideal for knitters. Even beginning knitters who haven't ventured beyond simple scarves can be ensured success with the first attempt. Think of the kimono as five large rectangular scarves—one for the back, one for each half of the front, and one for each sleeve. The only difference is that the rectangles are sewn (or in some cases, knitted) together. Experienced knitters can hone their skills by working intricate color or stitch patterns or by adding fine embellishments. Whatever your knitting expertise and whatever your shape, you'll find a knitted kimono a classic and sophisticated alternative to the traditional Western cardigan or jacket.

PARTS OF A KIMONO

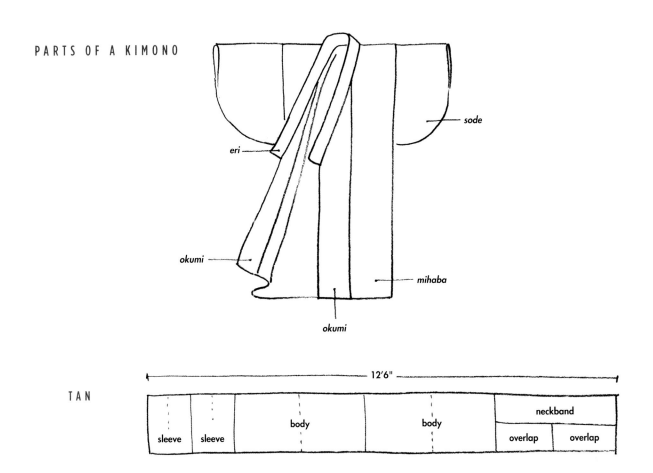

eri

sode

okumi

mihaba

okumi

TAN

12'6"

sleeve	sleeve	body	body	neckband	
				overlap	overlap

CONSTRUCTION

Kimono are generally constructed from rectangular pieces of fabric in standard widths. A bolt of cloth, called a tan, is cut into seven straight pieces: two long body panels, two sleeves, two overlaps, and a neckband. A standard tan is about 14" (35.5 cm) wide and 12½ yards (11.5 m) long and will make one ankle-length kimono. The body panels (mihaba) are seamed (by hand) at the center back and sides, with an opening at the center front. There are no shoulder seams. One overlap (okumi) is sewn to each front panel. The neckband (eri) is a folded strip of fabric that is attached to the front overlaps and around the neckline. It generally reaches about a third of the way down each side of the center front. Sleeves (sode) are the full width of the bolt and are sewn to the sides of the body.

Very little fabric is wasted in the making of a kimono. If the garment needs to be adjusted for a smaller body, deep seams are sewn along the sides and the extra-wide selvedges remain uncut on the inside of the garment. Throughout the ages, various parts have been widened or narrowed, lengthened or shortened, and otherwise subtly altered. Nevertheless, the technique of cutting a single bolt of cloth into seven rectangular pieces and stitching those pieces together without further shaping remains unchanged.

The spare shape of the kimono translates beautifully into knitted fabric. Cast on the number of stitches needed for the desired width of each rectangle, then knit for the desired length. Along the way, take a cue from Japanese artisans and add your own expressions of color, texture, and embellishment. Then sew the pieces together (by hand, just like the Japanese), and enjoy a garment that never goes out of fashion.

The Meaning of Kimono

In a traditional sense, the particular color, cut, and design of a kimono conveys social messages: gender, life/death, season, age, formality or occasion, and propriety. A kimono worn by a man is generally more conservative in both pattern and color—black, brown, gray, or dark blue—while a woman's kimono is a showcase for pattern and color. Bright colors are typically worn by young women, while more subdued colors are associated with maturity. In life, a kimono is always lapped left over right; for burial only is it lapped right over left. Understandably, an unlined, light open-weave silk kimono is worn in the summer months, while a lined, quilted hanten is saved for the winter season. The type of fabric, placement of design, and inclusion of crests can indicate a sense of formality. In a more abstract sense, the cut of a kimono can reflect an awareness of social etiquette. In Japan, where the nape is an erotic part of the body, the collar is worn closer to the nape for young, shy, and inexperienced females. The farther away the collar is from the nape, the greater the statement of maturity, sophistication, and even sensuality. Sleeve length implies gender, formality, and age. In traditional kimono, the depth of the sleeve from shoulder to armhole signifies social responsibility. An adult male, who has the most responsibility, wears the shallowest sleeves. An unmarried female, who is considered to hold the least responsibility, wears deep sleeves that can reach all the way to the floor (called furisode).

As contemporary knitters, we're free to adapt or ignore any of these guidelines. Today's fashions encourage a play of contradictions—the finest silk is at home with faded blue jeans; cut-and-slash jackets are paired with designer dresses on fashion runways. Take inspiration from the traditional or break away into your own design ideas.

DESIGNATION OF SLEEVE LENGTH

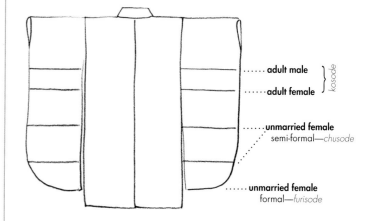

adult male ⎫
adult female ⎭ *kosode*

unmarried female
semi-formal—*chusode*

unmarried female
formal—*furisode*

A BRIEF HISTORY
OF THE KIMONO

In ancient and primitive Japan, clothing can be traced back to the influential continent of China. No complete garments have been preserved, but from priests' robes and paintings it is possible to reconstruct the style of dress up to and through the Nara period (645–794). Upper and lower garments with a rectangular cut and overlapping closure were in evidence, along with front and back skirts, and sashes, scarves, and stoles draped or wrapped around the body. By the ninth century the kosode, the archetypal kimono, was born. Communication ties with China were cut by then and Japan took the opportunity to evolve its own unparalleled statement of ethnic dress. The kimono has a rich and complex narrative—perhaps more than any other culture in history, the artistry and aesthetic beauty of kimono are tied to the changing political landscape and interconnected rules of society.

JUNIHITO

OSODE

SUIKAN

KOSODE

Heian Period (794–1185)

The Heian period marked the age of osode, which translates literally to "large sleeves." During this time, formal dress was a spectacular display of colorful layers called junihito (juni means "twelve"; hito means "unlined robes"). Noble women of the court took this concept to voluminous proportions, often wearing more than twelve layers of rather stiffly woven silk osode—each one a different color—layered on top of one another in a lavish visual display. The large, loose sleeves of osode had side wrist openings equal to the entire depth of the sleeve, allowing each layer to show through. The layers were also visible at the neckline and along the front edges where they swept back in beautiful curves. Specific color combinations held special meaning that related to the spirits of nature, including the seasons, geographic directions, personal virtues, and earthly elements. In paintings of the period, Heian beauties are almost completely enveloped in the billowing folds of their garments. Osode are still used in the imperial court for ceremonies and theatrical performances, such as bugaki (masked dance) and Noh dramas.

Commoners during the Heian period wore suikan, a garment having a double width of fabric for the sleeves with a cord used to draw up the sleeve opening. The suikan also featured side slits, open from hem to waist, to accommodate movement and allow the garment to be tucked into pleated pants called hakama.

The outermost robe of the junihito was a decorative large-sleeved robe called uchige. The innermost robe—the kosode—was a plain white undergarment with small sleeves made of simple plain-weave fabrics (commonly ramie and silk). During Japan's middle ages (1185–1868), kosode shifted from private to public view and, as such, were made from more elaborate fabrics such as silk twills (aya-ori), figured satin (rinzu), and crepes (chirimen). The basic shape of kosode has remained unchanged since the late Heian period, but fabric design and embellishment techniques have undergone many innovations in response to a series of all-embracing political changes. Kosode became the canvas on which Japanese artisans lavished their most creative visions.

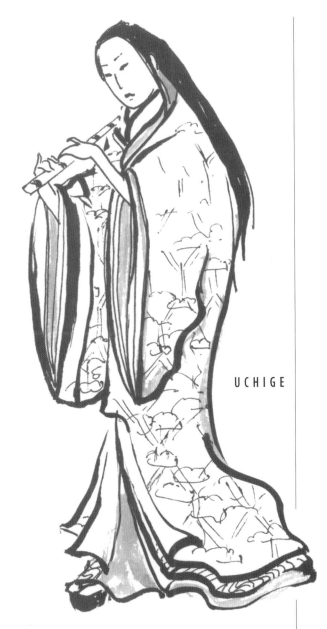

UCHIGE

Kamakura Period (1185–1333)

During the Kamakura period, the military class came to power and the capital was moved from the traditional central imperial seat of power in Kyoto to Kamakura in eastern Japan. All aspects of extravagant and opulent court life were replaced by a more restrained existence. The multilayered junihito was replaced by simpler ensembles of perhaps just one or two layers. Elaborate dress was reserved for warriors, who wore a two-piece hitatare under their armor, made from brocades decorated with floral designs, figured silks, and tie-dyed fabrics.

HITATARE

Moromachi Period (1333–1563)

The Ashiga dynasty of the shoguns dominated the Muromachi period, during which time the samurai ruled the military. The uchikake was the most elaborate outer garment of the kosode style, with small wrist openings, worn by upper class women of the ruling military class. Hitatare was the standard garment worn by males and motifs woven or dyed into the fabric evolved into larger-scale and more flamboyant patterns. The family crest, called a mon, became a popular ornamental feature as a way of establishing a clan or family (similar to a coat of arms) or as a way to honor and identify a particular accomplishment. A mon is a roundel encircling a stylized design of a traditional theme, such as flowers, bamboo, or fans. In a graduating scale of formality, a kimono may have one, three, or five crests. A single crested kimono displays the mon at the mid-back a few inches below the neckband. A three-crested kimono adds one to the back of each sleeve. A five-crested kimono adds one to each side of the front, placed just below the collarbone. Crests are not placed on komon, or small all-over patterning, kimono. Crests may be placed on asymmetrically decorated kimono, but most formal of all is the unpatterned monochrome kimono with five crests.

CRESTS

Ivy Crest

Triple Comma Crest

Bamboo Crest

HAORI

UCHIKAKE

Momoyama Period (1563–1615)

The brilliant Momoyama period marked a short-lived but extraordinary interval between war and peace during which opposites vied for aesthetic supremacy. Counterpoints like gold and straw or sophistication and rusticity were paired in equal measure—monumental castles and rustic teahouses were built; paintings ranged from spectacular audience-room masterpieces to intimate monochromatic works. During this period, elegant textiles were created in the pictorial *tsujigahana* style that combined a number of techniques, including *shibori* (resist dyeing), *kaki-e* (brush painting with sumi ink), *surihaku* (gold or silver leaf stenciling), and/or *huihaku* (embroidery) to dye fabrics, define lines, and create shadings.

During this time, fabrics began to be imported from the Chinese Ming dynasty, inspiring the Japanese to weave figured damasks, satins, and crepe silks for themselves. The more supple fabrics displaced stiff, heavy brocades and made way for an outpouring of artistic creativity in textile design. Cultivated cotton became widely available and commoners began to favor it over the traditional resilient but stiff bast fibers like hemp, flax, and ramie. A new design aesthetic emerged that featured dynamic asymmetry, irregular forms, and sweeping curves that defined a new artistic concept of space much like a painter might define a new compositional arrangement on a canvas.

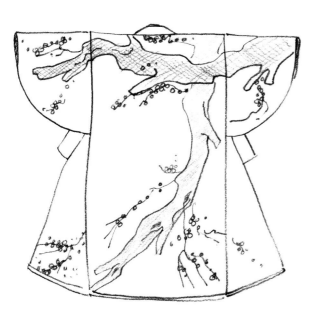

KANBUN STYLE

Edo Period (1600–1867)

The Edo period was named after the city of Edo (modern Tokyo), where the Tokugawa shoguns had their new seat of government. With the momentum of the Momoyama period, there was a rather seamless transition and continuation of artistic expression with the style of clothing that we generally think of today as traditional Japanese. Design expression expanded with the basic techniques of shibori, surihata (shibori-style resist using stencil patterns), embroidery, and parital nurizome (brush painting with dyes). During the early stages of the period (i.e., the mid-seventeenth century), the *Kanbun* kosode was in fashion. Fabric designs of earlier periods that had featured motifs and repetitive patterns densely compacted in an allover manner gave way to large abstract areas of color, dapple tie-dye, embroidery, and metallic leaf in bold sweeping diagonals on the back of kosode, extending from the right shoulder to the left skirt. The dramatic early Kanbun kosode style culminated in Genroku (1688–1704), a fleeting fad tucked into the Edo period. The nurizome brush-painting method gradually evolved into the yuzen dyeing technique, in which fine free-form resist lines produced crisp outlines of sharply defined areas of color. Yuzen was a more painterly technique that encouraged a fluid freedom of expression. Pictorial possibilities abounded with endless possibilities for color, shape, and shading. This dyeing technique unleashed a virtual revolution in Japanese textiles.

The lavish and radiant Genroku yuzen did not last, however. The Confucian-inspired ruling class banned the exuberantly colored, stunning oversize patterns in favor of a darker, more sophisticated aesthetic called iki. The pendulum once again shifted away from the obvious to the subtle, from bright colors to dark, and from jumbo free-form designs to petite pattern repeats.

It's safe to say that the kosode blossomed as an eloquent expression of Japanese culture and art during the entire span of the Momoyama and Edo periods. Drawing images from nature, literature, and everyday life, kosode designers could turn any subject into a decorative motif. Textile production reached its highest level of accomplishment in weaving techniques and design, and during this time woven patterns were replaced by dyed patterns of equal beauty at less expense. The dye work allowed a free and graphic style that more closely represented the inherent beauty of nature, a beauty that the Japanese welcomed into every aspect of their lives.

Kosode designs from the sixteenth to nineteenth centuries embody the best of the Japanese decorative style in a balance of opposites: expressive but not sentimental; filling the ground or space but not overcrowding it; delicate without rigid symmetry. Kosode designs during this period embody every artistic and technical accomplishment in weaving, dyeing, and embroidery, derived from long traditions of painting and crafts.

Contemporary Dress

In the mid-nineteenth century, kosode faced its first real competition with the appearance of Western clothing. But instead of being replaced with European-style clothing, the rich style, fabric, and design that had been associated with kosode for centuries were embraced as different and distinct. During the half century of the Meiji emperor's reign (1868–1912), the Japanese distilled their entire history into their ethnic dress. They replaced the term kosode with the word kimono ("object of wear") to represent the essence of Japanese culture that lives in this unique garment.

With the influx of Western clothing, there arose a vocabulary to define it as apart from Japanese clothing. Wafuku is Japanese; yofuku is Western. Wafuku is either noragi (working wear) or kimono. Kimono is either fundangi (everyday wear) or haregi (formal wear). Japanese men's clothing became known as yofuku, since they more readily adopted the European style of dress. Women continued to wear kimono well into the mid-twentieth century. Western clothing has now been adopted by the general Japanese population, but kimono continue to be worn for all occasions, from everyday work to formal celebrations and festivals. At the same time, the kimono style has expanded throughout the world where it is becoming a part of everyday dress everywhere.

We can honor the millennium of Japanese Kimono tradition by knitting them, and expressing in a contemporary way, our own interpretation of their beauty.

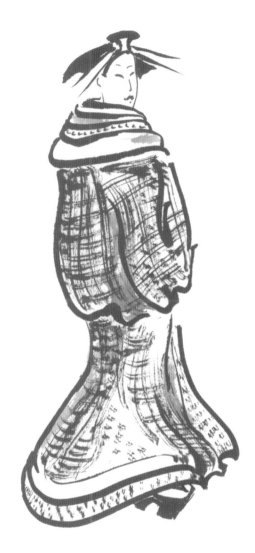

IKI KIMONO

DESIGN YOUR OWN KIMONO

The basic rectangular shape of a kimono makes it the easiest of all garments to design for knitting. Choose a yarn, knit a generous gauge swatch to determine the number of stitches you get per inch of knitting, do a few simple calculations, follow the schematics here, and you're on your way.

Choose a Yarn

You can have a lot of fun here. From rugged wool to drapey silk, from chunky to fine, to anything in between—any yarn will work.

Determine Your Gauge

Knit a generous gauge swatch (at least 6" [15 cm] square) with the yarn, needles, and stitch pattern you plan to use for your project. Wash the swatch as you plan to wash your finished kimono. When the swatch is thoroughly dry, place it on a flat surface and measure the number of stitches across 4" (10 cm) of knitting width. Divide that number by 4 to get the number of stitches per inch of knitting. Don't forget to include partial stitches—just one-half of a stitch in 4" can translate to several inches in the total circumference of the kimono. Measure the number of rows in the same way.

Determine Your Stitch Counts

Translate the measurements on the schematics below into number of stitches and rows by multiplying those numbers by your stitch and row gauge.

BACK

25 inches x_____ stitches/inch = _____ stitches to cast on

28 inches x _____ rows/inch = _____ rows to work to bind off

FRONT (MAKE 2 THE SAME)

9 inches x _____ stitches/inch = _____ stitches to cast on

28 inches x _____ rows/inch = _____ rows to work to bind off

SLEEVE (MAKE 2 THE SAME)

12 inches x _____ stitches/inch = _____ stitches to cast on

30 inches x _____ rows/inch = _____ rows to work to bind off

3 inches x _____ stitches/inch = _____ stitches to cast on

63 inches x _____ rows/inch = _____ rows to work to bind off

Note: The neckband should be stretched slightly for a tidy fit.

Make Your Own Variations

It's easy to add your own flavor by adding stitch or color patterns. Choose garter stitch or seed stitch or simple stripes for an easy kimono that requires no edge finishing. Choose Fair Isle or intarsia color work for more involved visual excitement. Add a hem or noncurling stitch to the edges of a stockinette stitch kimono. Adjust the length of the body pieces to long coat or short bolero. Make the sleeve deep and long or short and narrow. Once you're comfortable knitting the simple rectangular shapes, add rounded or asymmetrical shaping to the lower body, sleeves, or neckline. Add details like embroidery or a knit-cord knot closure. Before long, you'll be designing your own kimono intrigue.

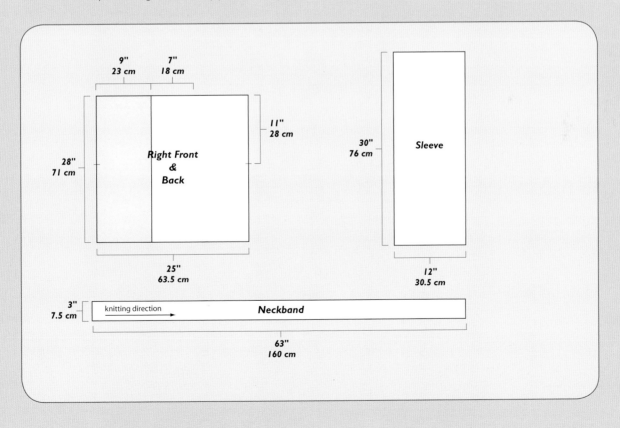

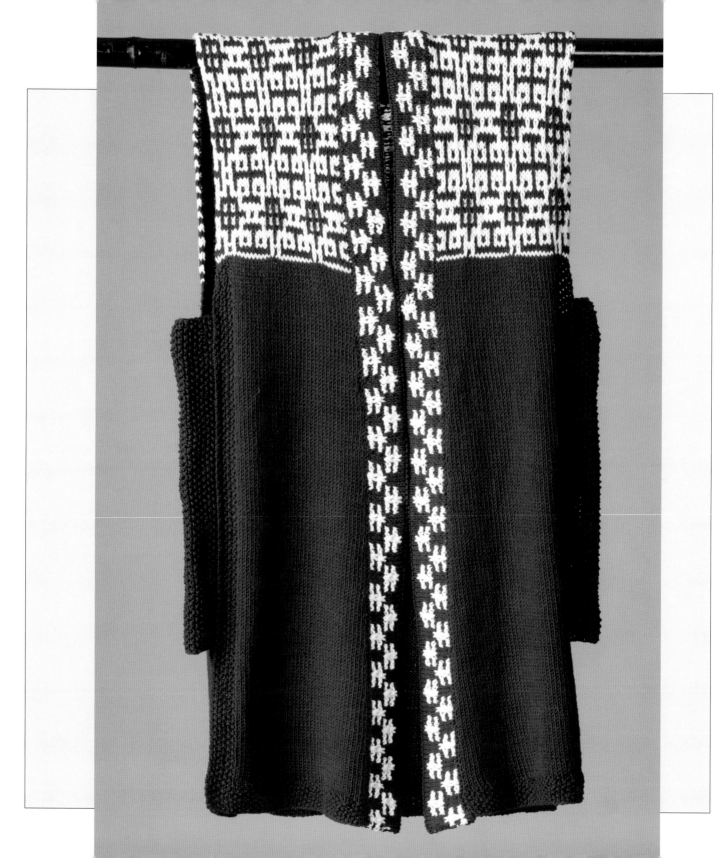

Katsuri Sodenashi

Ikat is the Malay word known worldwide for the process

called *katsuri* in Japanese. Katsuri is a thread-resist technique that we recognize as hazy white patterns reserved on a deep indigo ground. Ranging from simple mottled effects to abstract geometric motifs and free-form representations of nature's plant life, katsuri textiles are admired for the skill, ingenuity, and creative imagination they express.

Most widely known as a folk craft, katsuri textiles were woven at home primarily out of cotton. The weaving required command of technique, proficiency, and patience but needed few tools beyond the two-harness, back-tensioned loom used historically throughout Japan. The pattern is dyed into sections of the thread lengths before it is woven. Warp or weft alone may carry the pattern, or the pattern may be created by the intersection of dyed warp and weft.

Sodenashi was a common item of work apparel—a simple straight vest, with or without a collar strip. I let katsuri inspire me for the front and back yoke on this medium-length sleeveless cotton tunic, expressed in a slip-stitch pattern.

MATERIALS

FINISHED SIZE
About 55½" (141 cm) in circumference—53¼" (135.5 cm) garment plus a 2¼" (5.5 cm) space at center front—and 36" (91.5 cm) in length.

YARN
Worsted weight (#4 Medium).

Shown here: Cascade Sierra (80% cotton, 20% wool; 192 yd [176 m]/100 g): #66 indigo (MC), 8 hanks; #01 white (CC), 2 skeins.

NEEDLES
Size 8 (5 mm): 32" (80 cm) circular (cir). Adjust needle size if necessary to obtain the correct gauge.

NOTIONS
Stitch holders; tapestry needle.

GAUGE
18 stitches and 24 rows = 4" (10 cm) in stockinette stitch.

KATSURI SODENASHI

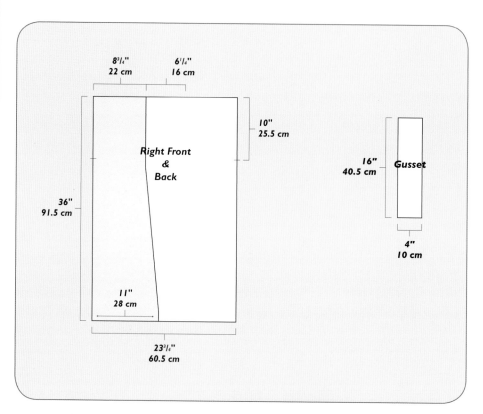

8³/₄"
22 cm

6¹/₄"
16 cm

10"
25.5 cm

Right Front
&
Back

36"
91.5 cm

11"
28 cm

23³/₄"
60.5 cm

16"
40.5 cm

Gusset

4"
10 cm

BACK

With MC, CO 107 sts. **Next row:** *K1, p1; rep from * to last st, k1. Rep the last row (seed st) until piece measures 1½" (3.8 cm) from CO, ending with a WS row. Cont as foll:

Row 1: (RS) [K1, p1] 3 times, knit to last 6 sts, [p1, k1] 3 times.

Row 2: [K1, p1] 3 times, purl to last 6 sts, [p1, k1] 3 times.

Rep Rows 1 and 2 until piece measures 26" (66 cm) from CO, ending with a RS row.

Yoke

With CC, purl 1 (WS) row. Cont as foll:

Row 1: (RS) With MC, k4, *sl 1, k1, sl 1, k9; rep from * to last 7 sts, sl 1, k1, sl 1, k4.

Row 2 and all WS rows: Using the same color as the preceding RS row, purl all the sts that were knitted on the preceding row and slip with yarn in front (wyf) all the sts that were slipped in the preceding row.

Rows 3 and 23: With CC, *k3, sl 1; rep from * to last 3 sts, k3.

Rows 5 and 21: With MC, k1, *k1, sl 1; rep from * to last 2 sts, k2.

Rows 7 and 19: With CC, *k5, sl 1; rep from * to last 5 sts, k5.

Rows 9 and 17: With MC, k2, *sl 1, k5; rep from * to last 3 sts, sl 1, k2.

Rows 11 and 15: With CC, k3, *sl 1, k1, sl 1, k1, sl 1, k7; rep from * to last 8 sts, sl 1, k1, sl 1, k1, sl 1, k3.

Row 13: With MC, k1, *k9, sl 1, k1, sl 1; rep from * to last 10 sts, k10.

Row 24: Rep Row 2.

Rep Rows 1–24 two more times—piece measures about 36" (91.5 cm) from CO. Place sts on holder.

LEFT FRONT

With MC, CO 49 sts. **Next row:** *K1, p1; rep from * to last st, k1. Rep the last row until piece measures 1½" (3.8 cm) from CO, ending with a WS row. Cont as foll:

Row 1: (RS) [K1, p1] 3 times, knit to last 3 sts, ssk, k1—1 st dec'd.

Row 2: Purl to last 6 sts, [p1, k1] 3 times.

Cont in seed st and St st as established, dec 1 st at end of RS row in this manner every 14th row 9 more times—39 sts rem. Cont even in patt until piece measures 26" (66 cm) from CO, ending with a RS row.

Yoke

With CC, purl 1 (WS) row. Cont as foll:

Row 1: (RS) With MC, k4, *sl 1, k1, sl 1, k9; rep from * to last 11 sts, sl 1, k1, sl 1, k8.

Row 2 and all WS rows: Using the same color as the preceding RS row, purl all the sts that were knitted in the preceding row and slip wyf all the sts that were slipped in the preceding row.

Rows 3 and 23: With CC, *k3, sl 1; rep from * to last 3 sts, k3.

Rows 5 and 21: With MC, k1, *k1, sl 1; rep from * to last 2 sts, k2.

Rows 7 and 19: With CC, *k5, sl 1; rep from * to last 3 sts, k3.

Rows 9 and 17: With MC, k2, *sl 1, k5; rep from * to last st, k1.

Rows 11 and 15: With CC, k3, *sl 1, k1, sl 1, k1, sl 1, k7; rep from *.

Row 13: With MC, k1, *k9, sl 1, k1, sl 1; rep from * to last 2 sts, k2.

Row 24: Rep Row 2.

Rep Rows 1–24 two more times—yoke measures about 10" (25.5 cm). Place sts on holder.

RIGHT FRONT

With MC, CO 49 sts. **Next row:** *K1, p1; rep from * to last st, k1. Rep the last row until piece measures 1½" (3.8 cm) from CO, ending with a WS row. Cont as foll:

Row 1: (RS) K1, k2tog, knit to last 6 sts, [p1, k1] 3 times—1 st dec'd.

Row 2: [K1, p1] 3 times, purl to end.

Cont in seed st and St st as established, dec 1 st at beg of RS row in this manner every 14th row 9 more times—39 sts rem. Cont even in patt until piece measures 26" (66 cm) from CO, ending with a RS row.

Yoke

With CC, purl 1 (WS) row. Cont as foll:

Row 1: (RS) With MC, k8, *sl 1, k1, sl 1, k9; rep from * to last 7 sts, sl 1, k1, sl 1, k4.

Row 2 and all WS rows: Using the same color as the preceding RS row, purl all the sts that were knitted in the preceding row and slip wyf all the sts that were slipped in the preceding row.

Rows 3 and 23: With CC, *k3, sl 1; rep from * to last 3 sts, k3.

Rows 5 and 21: With MC, k1, *k1, sl 1; rep from * to last 2 sts, k2.

Rows 7 and 19: With CC, k3, sl 1, *k5, sl 1; rep from * to last 5 sts, k5.

Rows 9 and 17: With MC, k1, *k5, sl 1; rep from * to last 2 sts, k2.

Rows 11 and 15: With CC, *k7, sl 1, k1, sl 1, k1, sl 1; rep from * to last 3 sts, k3.

Row 13: With MC, k2, *sl 1, k1, sl 1, k9; rep from * to last st, k1.

Row 24: Rep Row 2.

Rep Rows 1–24 two more times—yoke measures about 10" (25.5 cm). Place sts on holder.

JOIN SHOULDERS

Place 107 back sts onto one needle and 39 right front sts onto another needle. With CC and RS tog, use the three-needle method (see Glossary, page 117) to BO 39 sts tog for right shoulder, then BO 29 back sts for back neck, then BO rem 39 back sts tog with 39 left front sts for left shoulder. Cut yarn and pull tail through rem st to secure.

FINISHING

Yoke Armhole Facing

With MC, RS facing, and beg at base of left front yoke, pick up and knit 86 sts along selvedge edge of front and back yoke. Purl 1 (WS) row. Work even in St st until facing measures 1" (2.5 cm) from pick-up row. BO all sts. With yarn threaded on a tapestry needle, use a whipstitch (see Glossary, page 124) to tack facing to WS of yoke every 3 to 4 sts. Rep for right armhole, beg at base of right back yoke.

Neckband

With MC and RS facing, pick up and knit 172 sts along right front edge, 29 sts across back neck, and 172 sts along left front edge—373 sts total. Knit 1 (WS) row. Cont as foll:

Row 1: (RS) With CC, k5, *sl 3 with yarn in back (wyb), k5; rep from *.

Row 2: With CC, k2, p1, k2, *sl 3 wyf, k2, p1, k2; rep from *.

Row 3: With MC, k2, *sl 1 wyb, k7; rep from * to last 3 sts, sl 1, k2.

Row 4: With MC, k1, p1, *sl 1 wyf, p7; rep from * to last 3 sts, sl 1, p1, k1.

Rows 5, 6, and 7: Rep Rows 1, 2, and 3.

Row 8: With MC, k1, purl to last st, k1.

Row 9: With CC, k1, *sl 3 wyb, k5; rep from * to last 4 sts, sl 3, k1.

Row 10: With CC, k1, *sl 3 wyf, k2, p1, k2; rep from * to last 4 sts, sl 3, k1.

Row 11: With MC, k6, *sl 1 wyb, k7; rep from * to last 7 sts, sl 1, k6.

Row 12: With MC, k1, p5, *sl 1 wyf, p7; rep from * to last 7 sts, sl 1, p5, k1.

Rows 13, 14, and 15: Rep Rows 9, 10, and 11.

Row 16: With MC, k1, purl to last st, k1.

Rows 17 and 18: With MC, knit (turning ridge).

With MC, work even in St st for 6 rows.

Row 1: (RS) With CC, k5, *sl 3 wyb, k5; rep from *.

Row 2: With CC, p5, *sl 3 wyf, p5; rep from *.

Row 3: With MC, k2, *sl 1 wyb, k7; rep from * to last 3 sts, sl 1, k2.

Row 4: With MC, p2, *sl 1 wyf, p7; rep from * to last 3 sts, sl 1, p2.

Rows 5, 6, and 7: Rep Rows 1, 2, and 3.

Row 8: With MC, k2, *p1, k7; rep from * to last 3 sts, p1, k2.

BO all sts kwise. Fold facing at turning ridge to WS and whipstitch into place, catching the pick-up seam.

Side Gusset (make 2)

With MC, CO 17 sts. Work in seed st until piece measures 16" (40.5 cm) from CO. BO all sts in patt. Measure 1½" (3.8 cm) down from bottom edge of yoke on front and back and mark for gusset placement. Place top edge of gusset at marks and side edge 1 st underlapping front and back. (Gusset will not reach to lower edge of garment. Lower 8½" [21.5 cm] of side edge will remain free.) Use a whipstitch to sew in place on WS of garment.

Steam-block to measurements.

KATSURI **textiles are admired**

for the skill, ingenuity,

and creative imagination

they express.

Dogi

Stunningly beautiful striped patterns have woven their way

through kimono fashion for centuries. There are literally hundreds of variations of simple parallel-line stitch work. Stripes may be wide, narrow, paired, grouped in multiples, textured, or defined in a palette of two or more colors. The affluent used silk, and commoners used cotton. Folk textiles of the commoners were by nature utilitarian but by no means excluded decoration. Uniquely beautiful features are achieved through straightforward methods and are applied to garments that are functional and easy to move and work in, like the sleeveless tunic or vest.

This *dogi*, or vest, is knitted in one piece from side to side in a flat ribbon yarn. The yarn is a blend of rayon and cotton handpainted in the dark *shibui* colors of subdued browns and grays. Unlike traditional kimono silhouettes, I've shaped the armholes and lower edges of this vest into gentle and pleasing curves. However, the front opening hangs straight. The vest is worked in a button stitch textural pattern that produces subtle vertical stripes representative of many traditional kimono patterns. The edges are cleanly finished with knitted cord.

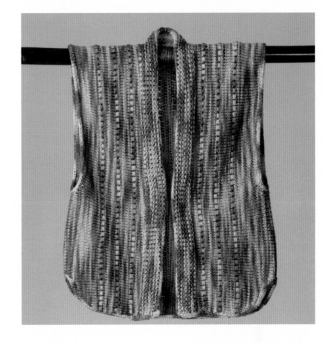

MATERIALS

FINISHED SIZE
About 42" (106.5 cm) in circumference—40" (101.5 cm) garment plus a 2" (5 cm) space at center front—and 22" (56 cm) in length.

YARN
Worsted weight (#4 Medium).
Shown here: Fiesta Meteor (50% rayon, 50% cotton; 180 yd [165 m]/4 oz): cinnamon, 6 skeins.

NEEDLES
Size 9 (5.5 mm): 24" (60 cm) circular (cir); spare size 9 (5.5 mm)

needle for finishing; size 10½ (6.5 mm): 32" (80 cm) cir; size 10 (6 mm) double-pointed (dpn). Adjust needle size if necessary to obtain the correct gauge.

NOTIONS
Small amount of waste yarn for provisional CO; size I/9 (5.5 mm) crochet hook; stitch holders; tapestry needle.

GAUGE
18 stitches and 24 rows = 4" (10 cm) in stockinette stitch on smallest needle.

DOGI

STITCH GUIDE
Button Stitch (worked over 2 sts)

Bring right needle in front of the left needle and insert tip between the second and third sts, wrap working yarn around right needle, draw up a loop (Figure 1), slip this loop pwise onto left needle tip (Figure 2), knit this st through the back loop (1 new st on right needle), slip the 2 wrapped sts (the first and second sts on left needle) pwise to right needle, then pass the new st on right needle over the 2 slipped sts and off needle (Figure 3).

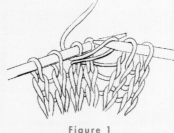

Figure 1

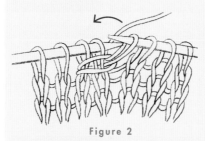

Figure 2

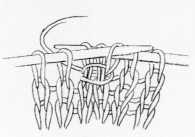

Figure 3

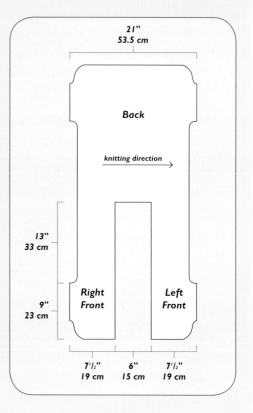

21"
53.5 cm

Back

knitting direction →

13"
33 cm

9"
23 cm

Right Front

Left Front

7½"
19 cm

6"
15 cm

7½"
19 cm

RIGHT FRONT/SIDE

With smallest needle, waste yarn and working yarn, use the crochet-chain method (see Glossary, page 118) to provisionally CO 27 sts, leaving a 24" (61 cm) tail of working yarn for later finishing. Purl 1 (WS) row. *Next row:* (RS) K1f&b (see Glossary, page 121), knit to last 2 sts, k1f&b, k1—2 sts inc'd. Purl 1 row. Rep the last 2 rows 2 more times—33 sts; piece measures about 1¼" (3.2 cm) from CO. Cut yarn, leaving an 8" (20.5 cm) tail. Place sts on holder.

RIGHT BACK/SIDE

CO and work same as right front/side but do not cut yarn and leave sts on needle—33 sts; piece measures about 1¼" (3.2 cm) from CO. With RS facing, use the cable method (see Glossary, page 118) to CO 110 sts for armhole—143 sts. With WS facing, purl 33 held right front/side sts—176 sts total. Cont in St st, use the cable method to CO 3 sts at beg of next 4 rows—188 sts. *Next row:* (RS) K1, use the backward-loop method (see Glossary, page 118) to CO 1 st, knit to last st, use the backward-loop method to CO 1 st, k1—2 sts inc'd. Purl 1 row. Rep the last 2 rows 4 more times—198 sts. *Next row:* (RS; button st row) K1, *work button st (see Stitch Guide) over next 2 sts; rep from * to last st, k1. Work 9 rows even in St st. Rep the last 10 rows once. Rep button st row. Purl 1 row. Work 4 rows even in St st, ending with a WS row—piece measures about 7½" (19 cm) from initial CO. With RS facing, k98 and place these sts on holder for right front, knit to end—100 sts rem for back. Work 3 rows even in St st. *Next row:* (RS; button st row) K1, *work button st over next 2 sts; rep from * to last st, k1. Work 9 rows even in St st. Rep the last 10 rows 2 more times. Work button st row. Purl 1 row. Work 2 rows even in St st, ending with a WS row—piece measures about 13½" (34.5 cm) from initial CO. With RS facing and waste yarn, use the crochet-chain method to provisionally CO 99 sts onto right needle for left front. With WS facing, purl these 99 sts. With RS facing, k98, k2tog (last st of left front tog with first st of back neck), knit to end—198 sts. Work 5 rows even in St st. *Next row:* (RS; button st row) K1, *work button st over next 2 sts; rep from * to last st, k1. Work 9 rows even in St st. Rep the last 10 rows 1 more time. Work button st row. Purl 1 row—piece measures about 17¾" (45 cm) from initial CO.

Shape Lower Edge

Next row: (RS) *K1, k2tog, knit to last 3 sts, ssk, k1—2 sts dec'd. Purl 1 row. Rep the last 2 rows 4 more times—188 sts rem. BO 3 sts at beg of next 4 rows—176 sts rem.

Shape Left Side/Front

(RS) K1, k2tog, k27, ssk, k1 (31 sts on right needle), place rem 143 sts on holder for left side/back. Purl 1 row. *Next row:* (RS) K1, k2tog, k25,

Unlike traditional kimono silhouettes, I've shaped the armholes and lower edges of this vest into gentle and pleasing curves.

ssk, k1—29 sts rem. Purl 1 row. *Next row:* K1, k2tog, k23, ssk, k1—27 sts rem. Purl 1 row. Place these sts on holder and cut yarn, leaving a 36" (91.5 cm) tail for grafting.

Shape Left Side/Back

Place 143 held left side/back sts onto needle. With RS facing, BO 110 sts for armhole (1 st on right needle), work rem 32 sts as k2tog, k27, ssk, k1—31 sts rem for left side/back. Purl 1 row. *Next row:* (RS) K1, k2tog, k25, ssk, k1—29 sts rem. Purl 1 row. *Next row:* K1, k2tog, k23, ssk, k1—27 sts rem. Purl 1 row.

Join Sides

Place left side/front sts onto spare needle, and with yarn threaded on a tapestry needle, use the Kitchener st (see Glossary, page 121) to join left side/front and left side/back sts tog. Remove provisional CO from right side/front and right side/back, placing sts onto two needles. Join right side as for left side.

FINISHING
Neckband

Place 98 held right front sts onto smallest needle. With largest needle and RS facing, [k2, k1f&b, k3, k1f&b] 14 times (126 sts for right front), pick up and knit 38 sts across back neck, remove waste yarn from provisional CO and place 98 left front sts onto smallest needle and work as [k2, k1f&b, k3, k1f&b] 14 times—290 sts total. Cont with largest needle as foll:
Row 1: (WS) *K2tog; rep from * to end—145 sts rem.
Row 2: (RS) *K1f&b; rep from * to end—290 sts.
Rep Rows 1 and 2 four more times, then rep Row 1 once more—6 garter ridges on RS. BO in knit-cord as foll: Place all sts on smallest needle. With attached yarn at lower right front edge, use the cable method to CO 3 sts. Cont with smallest needle, *k2, sl 1 kwise, sl 1 from neckband pwise, work these sts tog as for ssk, sl these 3 sts back to left needle; rep from * until all neckband sts have been BO—3 sts rem on right needle. Change to middle-size dpn and work as regular knit-cord (see Glossary, page 121) for 2 rows. Cont working knit-cord but attach it as you go from right to left along left front lower edge as foll: *K2, sl 1, pick up 1 st in knitted edge by inserting right needle into work and pulling a loop through, pass slipped st over picked up st and drop off needle, slide sts to opposite end of dpn; rep from *, picking up under 1 strand only of edge st and working to keep knitted fabric edge flat (about 2 rows of knit-cord for every 3 rows of garment along straight edges, about 1 row of knit-cord for every st along convex edge, and less than 1 row of knit-cord for every st along concave edge). Cont in this manner along the left front, back, and right front lower edges, ending at the right center front lower corner. Cut yarn, leaving a 10" (25.5 cm) tail. Thread tail on a tapestry needle and graft to CO edge as foll: Slide sts to opposite end of needle. Bring tapestry needle through first st pwise and leave st on needle, *bring tapestry needle down through center of first st on CO edge then up through second st, then kwise into first st on needle and remove st from needle, then insert tapestry needle into next st pwise and leave this st on the needle; rep from *, working across CO edge, and removing last st on needle after bringing tapestry needle through it kwise.
Block to measurements using the wet-towel method (see Glossary, page 117).

Indigo Noragi

Indigo is a common dyestuff, but the colors it produces

are anything but commonplace. Indigo-dyed cotton, native bast fibers, and tough wild silk were used in garments for the working class peasantry, or noragi. With a nod toward economy, mobility, warmth, and protection, functionality reigned supreme in Japanese folk clothing. Yet this did not preclude beauty. Working with materials easily accessible, beautiful craftwork emerged for pants, tops, leggings, vests, jackets, and aprons, as well as short kimono-shaped robes.

Here, I have taken artistic license with the basic shape of the kimono, folding the yoke to create the sleeves, adding pockets, using buttons as closure . . . but the basic kimono shape remains intact. I used a wave rib stitch that reads horizontally for the front yoke and back, then reads vertically where the fabric is folded for the sleeve. The remaining pieces are a bit of origami construction, but the result is an indigo flavored short silk jacket that is versatile and beautiful.

MATERIALS

FINISHED SIZE
About 45" (114.5 cm) in circumference and 22½" (57 cm) in length.

YARN
Worsted weight (#4 Medium).
Shown here: Reynolds Mandalay (100% silk; 98 yd [90 m]/50 g): #35 indigo, 15 skeins.

NEEDLES
Size 6 (4 mm): two 24" (60 cm) circular (cir). Adjust needle size if necessary to obtain the correct gauge.

NOTIONS
Tapestry needle; three 1⅛" x ½" (2.8 x 1.3 cm) buttons; size F/5 (3.75 mm) crochet hook.

GAUGE
17 stitches and 24 rows = 4" (10 cm) in stockinette stitch; 18 stitches and 26 rows = 4" (10 cm) in vertical wave rib pattern.

INDIGO NORAGI

1/1 LC: Knit into the back of the second st on left-hand needle but do not slip this st from the needle, bring right-hand needle in front of work and knit the first st on left needle, then slip both sts off tog.

1/1 RC: Knit the second st on left-hand needle by inserting right-hand needle from front to back but do not slip this st from the needle, knit the first st on the left needle, then slip both sts off tog.

VERTICAL WAVE RIB

(chart rows: 11, 9, 7, 5, 3, 1)

□ k on RS, p on WS

· p on RS, k on WS

□ pattern repeat

⊠ 1/1 RC: see Stitch Guide

⊠ 1/1 LC: see Stitch Guide

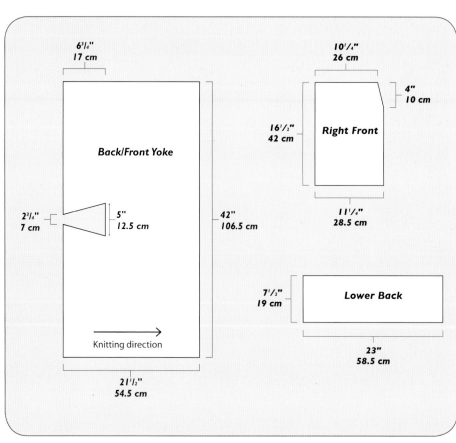

Back/Front Yoke

6³⁄₄" 17 cm

2³⁄₄" 7 cm

5" 12.5 cm

42" 106.5 cm

Knitting direction

21¹⁄₂" 54.5 cm

Right Front

10¹⁄₄" 26 cm

4" 10 cm

16¹⁄₂" 42 cm

11¹⁄₄" 28.5 cm

Lower Back

7¹⁄₂" 19 cm

23" 58.5 cm

LOWER BACK

CO 98 sts.

Row 1: (WS) P1, work Row 2 of Vertical Wave Rib chart (see page 36) across 96 sts, p1.

Row 2: (RS) K1, work Row 3 of chart across 96 sts, k1.

Row 3: P1, work Row 4 of chart across 96 sts, p1.

Row 4: K1, work Row 5 of chart across 96 sts, k1.

Row 5: Purl.

Cont in St st on all sts until piece measures 7½" (19 cm) from CO, ending with a WS row. With RS facing, BO all sts.

BACK/FRONT YOKE (worked from side to side)

CO 97 sts. Purl 1 (WS) row.

Row 1: (RS) K1 (selvedge st; work in St st), work Row 1 of chart to end.

Row 2: Work Row 2 of chart to last st, p1 (selvedge st).

Cont in this manner, working selvedge st in St st and 96 sts as charted until piece measures 18½" (47 cm) from CO, ending with a WS row.

Shape Left Front Neck

Cont in patt as established, work across 67 sts of back yoke, BO next 7 sts for front neck, work to end—23 sts rem for front yoke. Working on front yoke sts only, work 1 WS row. Keeping in patt, at neck edge (beg of RS rows), BO 7 sts once, then BO 8 sts 2 times. Cut yarn. With WS facing, rejoin yarn to 67 back yoke sts. Cont in patt until piece measures 23½" (59.5 cm) from CO, ending with Row 11 of chart.

Shape Right Front Neck

With spare cir needle and separate ball of yarn, CO 8 sts. Purl 1 (WS) row.

Row 1: (RS) Use the cable method (see Glossary, page 118) to CO 8 more sts, knit to end—16 sts.

Row 2: (WS) P3, k2, p4, k2, p4, k1.

Row 3: Use the cable method to CO 7 sts, k1, [1/1 RC (see Stitch Guide), k4] 3 times, 1/1 RC, k2—23 sts.

Row 4: P2, [k1, p1, k1, p3] 3 times, k1, p1, k1.

Row 5: Use the cable method to CO 7 sts, k1, [1/1 RC, k4] 4 times, 1/1 RC, k3—30 sts.

Row 6: Work Row 12 of chart across 30 front yoke sts, cont in patt across 67 back yoke sts—97 sts total.

Cont in patt until piece measures 18½" (47 cm) from neck join, ending with a WS row—piece measures 42" (106.5 cm) from CO. With RS facing, BO all sts.

RIGHT FRONT

CO 48 sts. Purl 1 (WS) row. Work even in St st until piece measures 12½" (31.5 cm) from CO, ending with a WS row. *Next row:* (RS) K1, k2tog, knit to end—1 st dec'd. Work 5 rows even. Rep the last 6 rows 3 more times—44 sts rem. Cont even until piece measures 16½" (42 cm) from CO, ending with a WS row. BO all sts.

LEFT FRONT

CO and work as for right front until piece measures 12½" (31.5 cm) from CO, ending with a WS row. *Next row:* (RS) Knit to last 3 sts, ssk, k1—1 st dec'd. Work 5 rows even. Rep the last 6 rows 3 more times—44 sts rem. Cont even until piece measures 16½" (42 cm) from CO, ending with a WS row. BO all sts.

LOWER FRONT POCKET (MAKE 2)

CO 50 sts.

Row 1: (WS) P1, work Row 2 of chart across 48 sts, p1.

Row 2: (RS) K1, work Row 3 of chart across 48 sts, k1.

Row 3: P1, work Row 4 of chart across 48 sts, p1.

Row 4: K1, work Row 5 across 48 sts, k1.

Row 5: Purl.

Cont even in St st until piece measures 7½" (19 cm) from CO. BO all sts.

FINISHING

With crochet hook and RS facing, single crochet (see Glossary, page 119) across top of pocket. Fasten off. Using the wet-towel method (see Glossary, page 117), block all pieces to measurements. Lightly steam edges if necessary to prevent curling. Let air-dry completely.

Assembly

Place back/front yoke RS down on a flat surface. Fold down the front yoke about 6¾" (17 cm) so that fold line is even with back neck BO, and fold up lower corner to front yoke edge, meeting side of back yoke to lower edge of front yoke forming sleeve cuff (Figure 1). With yarn threaded on a tapestry needle and using the invisible vertical to horizontal seam (see Glossary, page 122), sew seam from cuff edge along lower front yoke (about 9"–10" [23–25.5 cm]). Pin lower back to back yoke and sew seam from RS using invisible vertical to horizontal graft (Figure 2). Place piece on table so that RS of front yoke and WS of back yoke/lower back are facing up. Place the front in place and pin along yoke and sleeve. Place pocket on top of front and pin to lower back at side seam. With RS facing and using mattress st with a ½-st seam allowance, sew pocket to lower back, then cont seam by joining front to side of sleeve from lower sleeve edge to bottom of yoke using a 1-st seam allowance (Figure 3). Using invisible vertical to horizontal graft, sew front to front yoke (Figure 4). Fold pocket away from front. With WS of pocket and RS of front facing, use a whipstitch (see Glossary, page 124) to sew front to inside of seam of lower back/pocket (Figure 5). Fold pocket over front and steam press side seam to flatten (Figure 6). Whipstitch lower edges of pocket to front. Whipstitch top of pocket to front for 5" (12.5 cm) from center front (Figure 7).

Front Border

Mark first decrease row on front. With RS facing and beg at right center front lower edge, pick up and knit 54 sts (through pocket and front layers) to marked dec row, 48 sts along right neck edge, 22 sts across back neck, 48 sts along left front neck edge to corresponding dec row, and 54 along left front edge—226 sts total. Knit 7 rows—4 garter ridges on RS. *Buttonhole row:* (RS) K26, work one-row buttonhole over 3 sts (see Glossary, page 117), [k10, work buttonhole over 3 sts] 2 times, knit to end—3 buttonholes total. Knit 7 rows. With RS facing, work knit-cord BO as foll: Use the cable method to CO 3 sts. *K2, ssk, sl 3 sts back to left-hand needle; rep from * to end of row. To finish, pass second and third sts over the first and off the needle. Cut yarn and pull tail through rem st to secure.

Lay right front border over left front border and mark button placement, centered on left border. Sew buttons onto left front border.

Steam-block all seams and border.

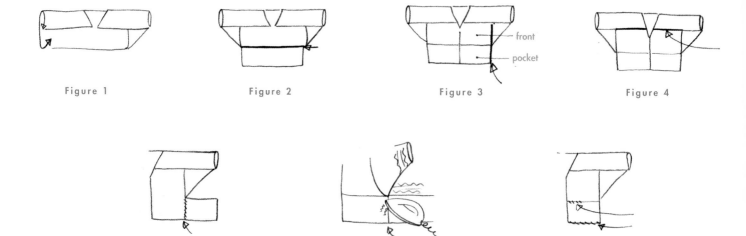

Figure 1   Figure 2   Figure 3   Figure 4

Figure 5   Figure 6   Figure 7

Uchikake is an elegant outer robe worn unbelted over kimono,

a style that originated during the Muromachi period. These robes usually have padded hems. They are worn today by brides as part of the traditional attire. Over the centuries of classical kimono fashion, there have been specific and defined zones of decoration. *Kata suso* is pictorial embellishment in the shoulder and hem areas. During the Meiji period (1868–1912), newly introduced analine dyes that produced a light, muted turquoise blue became common.

In a blending of attributes of various time periods of kimono history, I have created a kimono with clean graphic images of water in kata suso with a hint of the formal padded hem of the uchikake. Paradoxically, the somewhat mottled texture of the cotton gives the garment a more casual look than these formal elements would indicate. Yet, because of the blend of casual and formal, this kimono is at ease at both ends of the social spectrum.

MATERIALS

FINISHED SIZE
About 49" (124.5 cm) in circumference—48" (122 cm) garment plus a 1" (2.5 cm) space at center front)—and 40" (101.5 cm) in length.

YARN
Worsted weight (#4 Medium).
Shown here: Mission Falls 1824 Cotton (100% cotton; 84 yd [77 m]/50 g): #401 chicory (MC), 18 balls; #300 lichen (CC1), 8 balls; #103 pebble (CC2), 5 balls.

NEEDLES
Size 7 (4.5 mm): 24" (60 cm) circular (cir); spare needle of same size or slightly smaller for finishing. Adjust needle size if necessary to obtain the correct gauge.

NOTIONS
Stitch holders; tapestry needle; size E/4 (3.5 mm) crochet hook.

GAUGE
18 stitches and 27 rows = 4" (10 cm) in stockinette stitch.

LEFT BACK

With lichen, CO 55 sts. Knit 3 rows. Work Rows 1–70 of Waves Left Back and Front chart (page 44), beg and ending as indicated for left back. With chicory, cont even in St st until piece measures 40" (101.5 cm) from CO, ending with a WS row. Place sts on holder.

RIGHT BACK

With lichen, CO 55 sts. Knit 3 rows. Work Rows 1–70 of Waves Right Back chart (page 45). With chicory, cont in St st until piece measures 40" (101.5 cm) from CO, ending with a WS row. Place sts on holder.

LEFT FRONT

With lichen, CO 70 sts. Knit 3 rows. Work Rows 1–70 of Waves Left Back and Front chart, beg and ending as indicated for left front. With chicory, cont in St st, dec 1 st at end of next RS row, then every 10th row 3 more times—66 sts rem. Work 7 rows even, then dec 1 st at end of next (RS) row—1 st dec'd. Rep the last 8 rows 7 more times—58 sts rem. Cont even until piece measures 26" (66 cm) from CO, ending with a WS row.

Shape Neck

Dec 1 st at neck edge (end of RS rows) every 4th row 15 times—43 sts rem. Cont even until piece measures 40" (101.5 cm) from CO, ending with a WS row. Place sts on holder.

RIGHT FRONT

With lichen, CO 70 sts. Knit 3 rows. Change to St st, alternating 2 rows chicory with 2 rows lichen for 70 rows—piece measures about 10¾" (27.5 cm) from CO. Cont in stripe patt, dec 1 st at neck edge (beg of RS rows) on next row, then every 10th row 3 more times—66 sts rem. Work 7 rows even, then dec 1 st at beg of next (RS) row—1 st dec'd. Rep the last 8 rows 7 more times—58 sts rem. Cont even in patt until piece measures 26" (66 cm) from CO, ending with a WS row.

Shape Neck

Dec 1 st at neck edge (beg of RS rows) every 4th row 15 times—43 sts rem. Cont even until piece measures 40" (101.5 cm) from CO, ending with a WS row. Place sts on holder.

LEFT SLEEVE

With lichen, CO 18 sts. Purl 1 (WS) row. For the front of the sleeve, work Rows 1–74 of Waves Left Sleeve chart (page 46), using the cable method (see Glossary, page 118) to CO sts at beg of RS rows as indicated, beg with CO 5 sts on Row 1—60 sts after all sts have been CO. With chicory, cont even until piece measures 12" (30.5 cm) from last color change on Row 74, ending with a WS row. For the back of the sleeve, turn Waves Right Sleeve chart upside down and work Rows 1–79 of chart, binding off at beg of RS rows as indicated—18 sts rem. Work 1 WS row even. With RS facing, BO all sts.

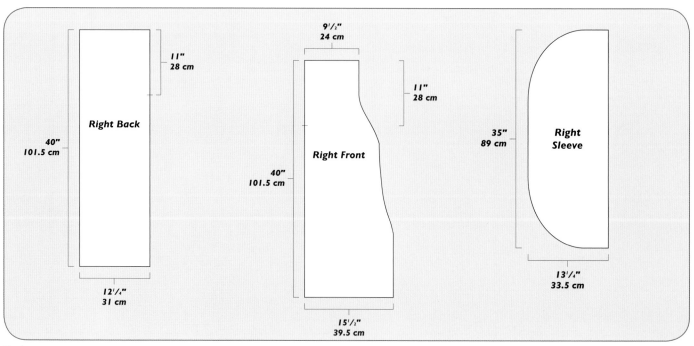

RIGHT SLEEVE

With lichen, CO 18 sts. For the front of the sleeve, work Rows 1–76 of Waves Right Sleeve chart (page 47), using the cable method to CO sts at beg of WS rows as indicated—60 sts after all sts have been CO. With chicory, cont even until piece measures 12" (30.5 cm) from last color change on Row 75, ending with a WS row. For the back of the sleeve, turn Waves Left Sleeve chart upside down and work Rows 1–79 of chart, binding off at beg of WS rows as indicated—23 sts rem. At beg of next WS row, BO 5 sts—18 sts rem. Knit 1 (RS) row. BO all sts.

FINISHING

Steam- or wet-towel block (see Glossary, page 117) all pieces to measurements. Let air-dry completely.

Assembly

Place all 43 right front sts on one needle and 55 right back sts on another needle with points toward the side edge and RS tog. Use the three-needle method (see Glossary, page 117) to BO 43 sts for right shoulder, then BO rem 12 back sts. Place 43 left front sts on one needle and 55 left back sts on another needle with points toward the side edge and RS tog. Use the three-needle method to BO 43 sts for left shoulder, then BO rem 12 back sts. With yarn threaded on a tapestry needle and using the mattress st for St st with a ½-st seam allowance (see Glossary,

page 123), sew side seams for 26" (66 cm) from lower edge. Sew center back seam. Fold sleeve with RS tog, meeting CO and BO edges. Measure 6" (15 cm) down from fold on curved edge to mark hand opening. With crochet hook, work slip-stitch seam along lower curved edge to that mark. Steam-press seam allowance to compress seam bulk and make a smooth curve. Turn sleeve right side out. Measure 11" (28 cm) down from shoulder seam along side edge of front and back. Mark 11" (28 cm) on each side of fold on sleeve. Pin sleeve to body, matching fold of sleeve to shoulder seam and matching 11" (28 cm) marks. Use the mattress st to sew sleeve to body.

Crochet Edging

With lichen, RS facing, and beg at right center front lower edge, work 1 row of single crochet (see Glossary, page 119) up right front, across back neck, and down left front edge. With chicory and RS facing, work 1 row of single crochet around sleeve hand opening.

Neckband

Measure 5½" (14 cm) down from shoulder seam along right and left center front edge and mark for neckband placement. With chicory and RS facing, pick up and knit 1 st in each sc along right front, back neck, and left front between markers—about 70 sts total. Work even in garter st for 1½" (3.8 cm), ending with a RS row. With WS facing, BO all sts kwise. Steam-block crochet edges from WS of garment. Let air-dry.

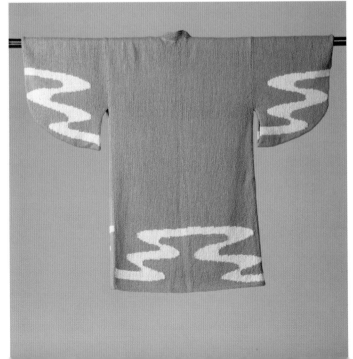

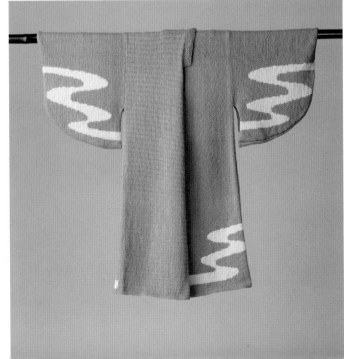

WAVES LEFT BACK AND FRONT

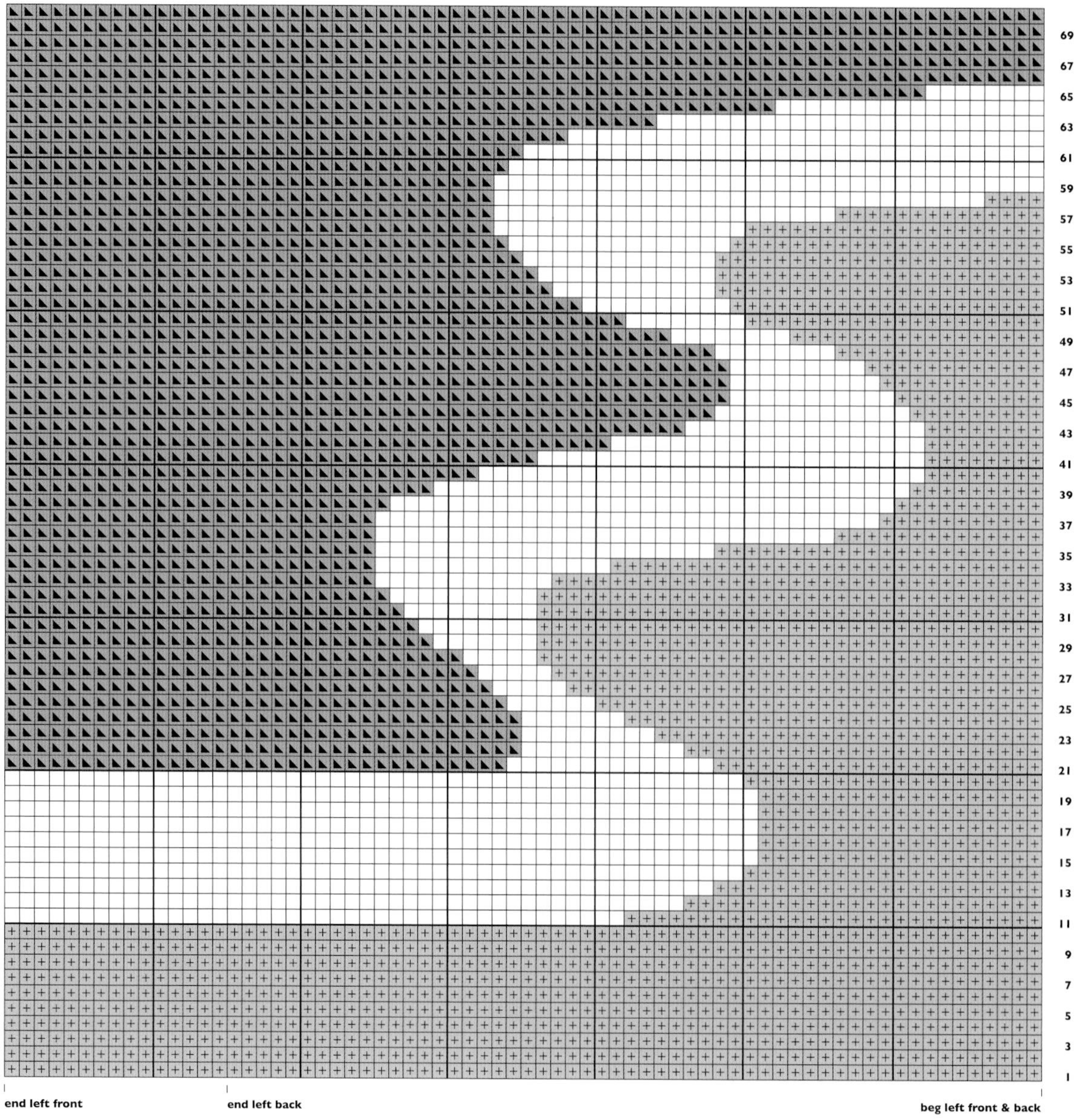

69
67
65
63
61
59
57
55
53
51
49
47
45
43
41
39
37
35
33
31
29
27
25
23
21
19
17
15
13
11
9
7
5
3
1

end left front   end left back   beg left front & back

- ◣ chicory
- ☐ pebble
- + lichen

69
67
65
63
61
59
57
55
53
51
49
47
45
43
41
39
37
35
33
31
29
27
25
23
21
19
17
15
13
11
9
7
5
3
1

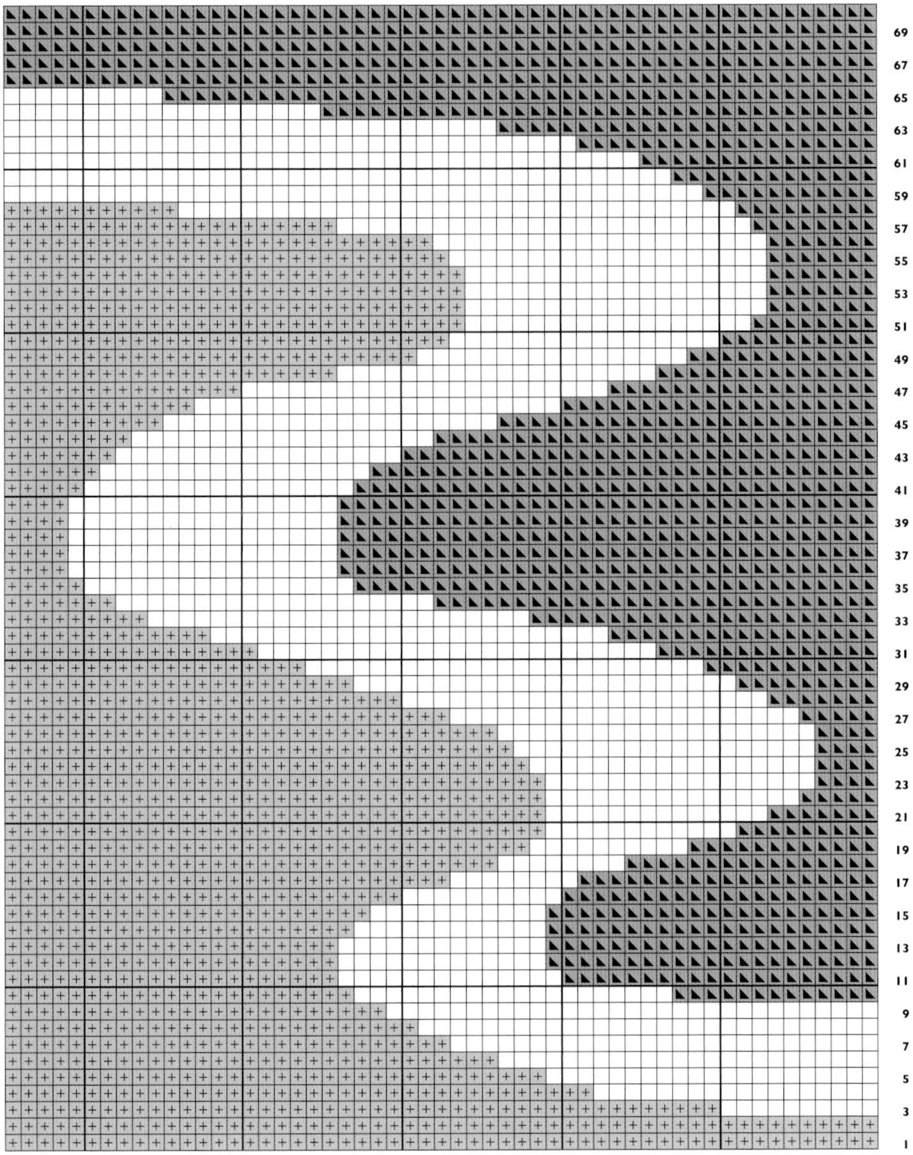

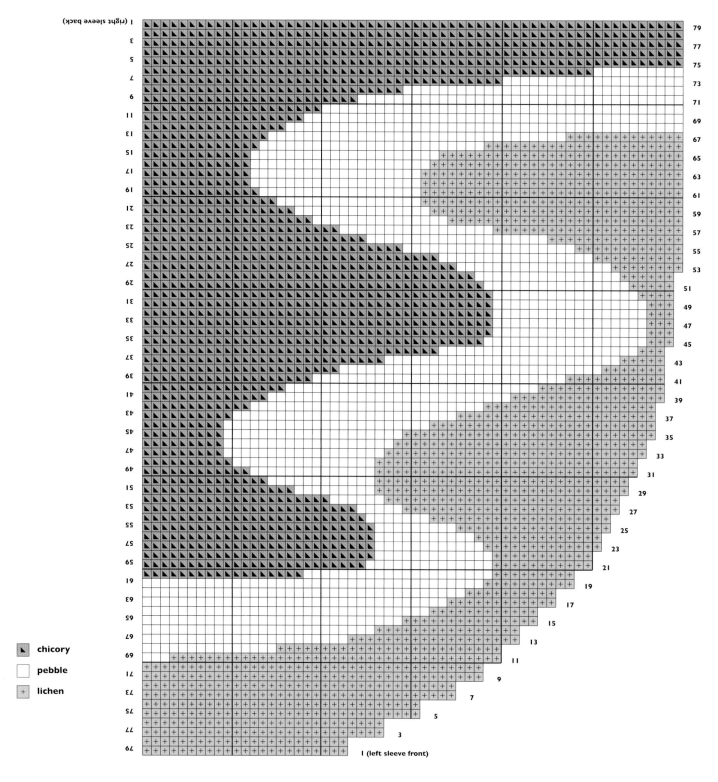

chicory

pebble

+ lichen

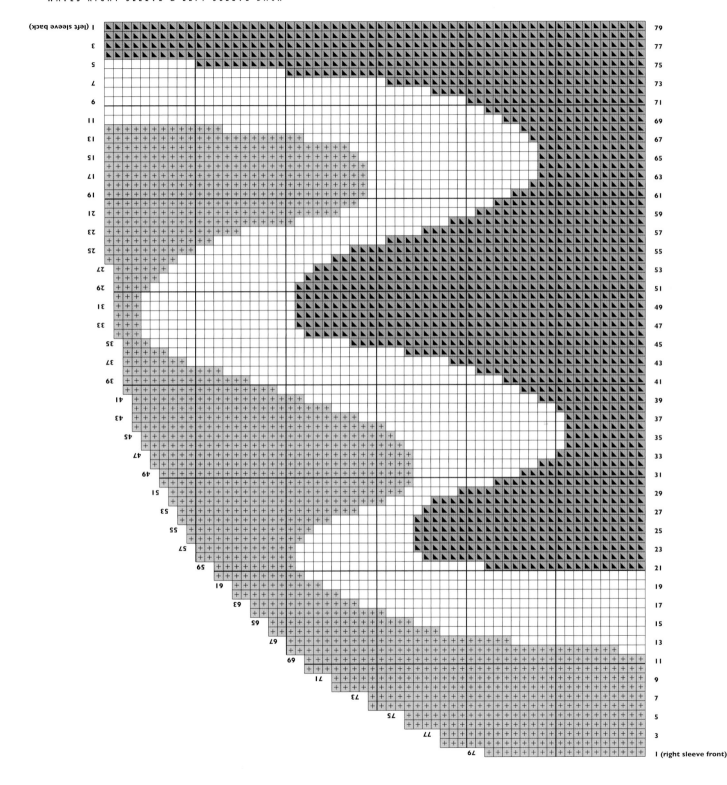

During the Edo period (1600–1867), the *chonin*, or urban artisans

and merchants, expanded their wealth through commerce in the burgeoning seaport of Osaka in western Japan. Far from the *bafuku* shogunal government in Edo (modern Tokyo), Osaka fashion and theater found ways to circumvent the governmental edicts to curb extravagant living. During the Genroku period (1688–1703), merchant patronage of outrageously elaborate textiles reached its peak. This is when *sogisode* emerged, an excessively long sleeve design with machete-shaped curved outer edges.

I took that curve and created full, deep sleeves that are shaped and gathered into smaller cuffs. Nature's range of color and texture provides the textural inspiration for this hip-length kimono. The crossover stitch evokes images of green grasses and reeds blowing and crossing in the wind. The handpainted bamboo fiber calls to mind the dyeing techniques used on kimono for centuries. The cuffs and neckband are faced with black to set off the subtle color and texture combination and give a hint of layering.

MATERIALS

FINISHED SIZE
About 50" (127 cm) in circumference and 28" (71 cm) in length (stretches to 34" [86.5 cm]).

YARN
Worsted weight (#4 Medium).

Shown here: Southwest Trading Company Bamboo (100% bamboo; 250 yd [229 m]/100 g): parrot (MC), 12 balls.

Southwest Trading Company Oasis (100% Soy Silk; 240 yd [219 m]/100 g): black (CC), 1 ball.

NEEDLES
Body and sleeves—size 6 (4 mm): 24" (60 cm) circular (cir); neckband—size 4 (3.5 mm): 24" (60 cm) cir. Adjust needle size if necessary to obtain the correct gauge.

NOTIONS
Cable needle (cn); open-ring markers (m); stitch holders; tapestry needle.

GAUGE
28 stitches and 34 rows = 4" (10 cm) with MC in pattern stitch on larger needle (see Note); 24 stitches and 34 rows = 4" (10 cm) with MC in stockinette stitch on larger needle.

REEDS & GRASSES

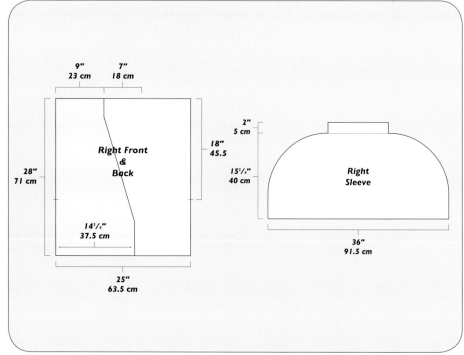

STITCH GUIDE

Pattern Stitch   (multiple of 4 stitches + 1)

Rows 1 and 5: (RS) *K2, sl 1 pwise, k1; rep from * to last st, k1.

Rows 2 and 6: P1, *p1, sl 1 pwise, p2; rep from *.

Row 3: *Sl 2 sts onto cn and hold in back of work, knit the sl st of 2 previous rows, k2 from cn, k1; rep from * to last st, k1.

Rows 4 and 8: Purl.

Row 7: K1, *k1, place sl st onto cn and hold in front of work, k2, k1 from cn; rep from *.
Repeat Rows 1–8 for pattern.

NOTE

● To test gauge, cast on 45 sts and work Rows 1–8 of pattern stitch until piece measures 6" (15 cm). Measure your gauge in the center 4" (10 cm) of the swatch.

BACK

With MC and larger needle, CO 175 sts. Purl 1 (WS) row. K1 (selvedge st; work in St st), place marker (pm), work Row 1 of patt st (see Stitch Guide) to last st, pm, k1 (selvedge st; work in St st). Working the first st and last st in St st and the center 173 sts in established patt, rep Rows 1–8, until piece measures about 28" (71 cm) from CO, ending with Row 4 or 8 of patt. Place sts on holder.

RIGHT FRONT

With MC and larger needle, CO 103 sts. Purl 1 (WS) row. Work first and last st in St st and center 101 sts in patt as for back until piece measures 6" (15 cm) from CO, ending with a WS row. *Dec row:* (RS) K1, k2tog, work in patt to end of row—1 st dec'd. Work 3 rows even in patt. Rep the last 4 rows 39 more times—63 sts rem. Cont even in patt until piece measures same as back, ending with Row 4 or 8 of patt. Place sts on holder.

LEFT FRONT

Work as for right front until piece measures 6" (15 cm) from CO, ending with a WS row. *Dec row:* (RS) Work in patt to last 3 sts, ssk, k1—1 st dec'd. Work 3 rows even in patt. Rep the last 4 rows 39 more times—63 sts rem. Cont even in patt until piece measures same as back, ending with Row 4 or 8 of patt. Place sts on holder.

JOIN SHOULDERS

Place 173 back sts onto one needle and 63 right front sts onto another needle. With RS tog, use the three-needle method (see Glossary, page 117) to BO 63 right front sts tog with 63 back sts for right shoulder, BO next 49 sts of back for back neck, then BO rem 63 back sts tog with 63 left front sts for left shoulder.

SLEEVES

Measure down 18" (45.5 cm) from shoulder seam on front and back and place markers for sleeve placement. With MC, larger needle, and RS facing, pick up and knit 216 sts between markers. Purl 1 (WS) row. (*Note:* Work decs as k1, k2tog, knit to last 3 sts, ssk, k1.) Work in St st, [dec 1 st each end of needle every 4th row once, then every 2nd row once] 22 times, ending with a WS row—128 sts rem. *Next row:* (RS) Change to smaller needle and *k2tog; rep from *—64 sts rem. Knit 1 (WS) row.

Cuff

Change to CC and knit 2 rows (1 garter ridge). Change to MC and knit 2 rows. Cont in St st until cuff measures 2" (5 cm) from last garter ridge,

ending with a RS row. Knit 1 WS row for turning ridge. Change to CC and dec 4 sts evenly spaced across next row—60 sts rem. Cont in St st for facing until piece measures 2" (5 cm) from turning ridge. BO all sts.

FINISHING

Front border and neckband

With MC, smaller needle, and beg at right center front lower edge, pick up and knit 30 sts to first neckline dec (about 6" [15 cm]), 121 sts to shoulder seam, 36 sts across back neck, 121 sts to first dec of left center front, and 30 sts to lower edge—338 sts total. Knit 1 (WS) row. Change to CC and knit 2 rows (1 garter ridge). Change to MC and knit 1 row. *Next row:* (WS) BO 30 sts kwise, knit to last 30 sts, BO rem sts kwise—278 sts rem. Cut yarn. With RS facing, reattach MC to first st. Cont in St st until piece measures 2" (5 cm) from last garter ridge, ending with a RS row. Knit 1 (WS) row for turning ridge. Change to CC and dec 10 sts evenly spaced—268 sts rem. Cont even in St st until piece measures 2" (5 cm) from turning ridge. BO all sts. Fold neckband facing to WS at turning ridge and whipstitch (see Glossary, page 124) in place.

Seams

With MC threaded on a tapestry needle and RS facing, use the mattress stitch (see Glossary, page 123) to sew side and sleeve seams. Fold cuff facings to WS at turning ridge and whipstitch in place.

Lightly steam-press seams.

Noragi, literally field wear, were rural garments woven from

bast (plant) fibers such as hemp and ramie, known collectively in Japan as *asa*. Depending on whether the threads were gleaned from stem or leaf, the fabric could be quite coarse or silky smooth. The most basic work clothes were made of extremely tough fabrics in plain, natural colors. At the other end of the spectrum is the hanten, a short kimono of a more polished cloth.

I have let natural colors, fibers, and flavor infuse the design of this kimono, with its simple stripes and warm, unbleached coloring. The fabric in this kimono is reflective of woven bamboo mats, the woven inner sole of zori sandals, and rice paper sliding screens. The fluid nature of the yarn in combination with the subtle garter-stitch texture makes a fabric with a fluid drape that is simultaneously elegant and casual. With a handful of basic beginning techniques, this kimono is a pleasure to knit and to wear. Naturally.

MATERIALS

FINISHED SIZE
About 50" (127 cm) in circumference—49" (124.5 cm) garment plus a 1" (2.5 cm) space at center front—and 28" (71 cm) in length. (*Note:* Kimono measures 23½" [59.5 cm] laying flat and extends to 28" [71 cm] due to flexibility of garter stitch and the weight of the yarn.)

YARN
Worsted weight (#4 Medium).

Shown here: Plymouth Linen Isle (50% cotton, 30% rayon, 20% linen; 86 yd [79 m]/ 50 g): #7009 maize, 14 balls; #7503 natural, 8 balls; #7471 herb, 4 balls.

NEEDLES
Size 7 (4.5 mm): 24" (60 cm) circular (cir); spare needle of same size or slightly smaller for three-needle bind-off. Adjust needle size if necessary to obtain the correct gauge.

NOTIONS
Open-ring markers; stitch holders or waste yarn; knitters' pins; tapestry needle.

GAUGE
18 stitches and 36 rows = 4" (10 cm) in garter stitch.

STITCH GUIDE

Color Sequence

Rows 1–14: Maize.

Rows 15 and 16: Natural.

Rows 17 and 18: Maize.

Rows 19–22: Natural.

Rows 23–26: Maize.

Rows 27 and 28: Natural.

Rows 29 and 30: Maize.

Rows 31 and 32: Herb.

Rows 33–36: Natural.

Repeat Rows 1–36 for color sequence.

NOTE

● The number of rows worked in each color is a multiple of two; all color changes occur on wrong-side rows. What is typically considered the wrong side of garter-stitch color changes will show on the right side of this garment.

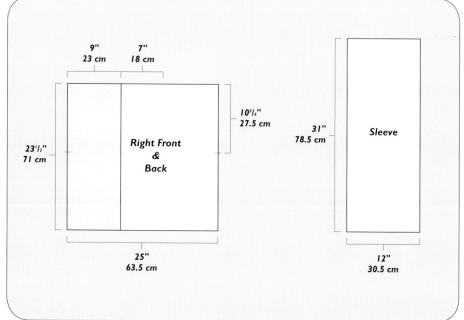

BACK

With maize, CO 112 sts. Work in garter st, rep Rows 1–36 of color sequence (see Stitch Guide) 5 times, then work Rows 1–32 once more—piece measures about 23½" (59.5 cm) from CO (but will stretch when worn). Place all sts on holder.

FRONTS

With maize, CO 40 sts. Working in garter st, rep color sequence as for back, ending with Row 32. Place all sts on holder. Make another front the same.

SLEEVES

With maize, CO 54 sts. Working in garter st, rep Rows 1–36 of color sequence 7 times, then work Rows 1–26 once more—piece measures about 31" (78.5 cm) from CO. BO all sts.

NECKBAND

With herb, CO 14 sts. Work even in garter st for 212 rows (106 ridges, same as on fronts). Place open-ring marker in piece to mark shoulder seam. Cont even in garter st until piece measures 7" (18 cm) from shoulder marker. Place another open-ring marker in work to mark second shoulder seam. Cont even in garter st for 212 more rows (106 ridges from second marker). BO all sts. *Note:* when knitting neckband, always add a new ball at the same edge. Sew that edge to front, reserving the clean edge for the finished edge.

FINISHING

Join Shoulders

Place 112 back sts onto one needle and 40 left front sts onto another needle. Hold the two pieces with WS tog (the side with the single color ridges) with left front on top of back. With herb, use the three-needle method (see Glossary, page 117) to BO 40 sts for left shoulder. Cont to BO the next 32 back sts, then use the three-needle method as before to BO rem 40 back sts tog with 40 right front sts for right shoulder. The BO will form a decorative ridge on the RS of the garment.

Side Seams

Pin front to back at side seams, matching the first three green stripes from lower edge. With maize threaded on a tapestry needle, use the mattress st for garter stitch (see Glossary, page 123) to sew side seams from lower edge towards shoulder, matching ridge for ridge and ending 5 ridges above the third green stripe.

Sleeve Seams

Fold sleeve in half at midpoint with RS tog. With maize threaded on a tapestry needle, use a whipstitch (see Glossary, page 124) to join CO to BO edges. Turn piece right side out and fold sleeve along the fourth green stripe (this will match the shoulder seam). Pin the edge of the sleeve that has all the color changes (the clean edge will form the cuff edge) to the front and back, matching green stripes (the maize/natural stripes will match on only one side of the garment). Beg at the eighth ridge above the lowest green stripe, use the mattress st for garter st to sew sleeves into armholes, ending at the eighth ridge above the other lowest green stripe; the lower 5" to 6" (12.5 to 15 cm) of the sleeve will rem unseamed.

Join Neckband

Pin the neckband onto garment, matching open-ring markers to shoulder seams, and matching lower edges of band and front. With herb and beg at lower front edge, use the mattress st for garter stitch to sew neckband to one front, matching garter ridges along front, then use a whipstitch to cont across the back neck, then use the mattress st to cont along the other front.

Weave in loose ends.

Lightly steam seams. Block to measurements.

The Kamakura period in the late twelfth century was an age

of military efficiency rather than courtly luxury. Leaders of two warrior clans rose to power and established a military government headquartered in Kamakura, far east of the imperial capital of Kyoto. The advent of a military government influenced dress styles. The frugality, simplicity, and discipline of Zen Buddhism appealed to fighting men, who saw the elaborate opulence and restrictive style worn by nobility as unsuitable for their active life. The new leaders adopted the suikan, a three-quarter-length upper garment that was tied at a small round neck and had very large sleeves. The suikan was always worn tucked into trousers.

I have kept the texture simple in my version to keep the focus on the unusual shape. The sleeves are wide (but not the suikan's equivalent of two full widths of the standard tan) and reach to the wrist. A drawstring running through the cable detail allows the sleeves to be gathered into a smaller opening at the cuff. The elegantly curved front opening is set off with a single garter ridge of bright orange. The small round neck is fastened with a Chinese knot. The intensity of the red yarn is relieved by the splashes of bright orange at the collar, cuff, and hem.

MATERIALS

FINISHED SIZE
About 50" (127 cm) in circumference and 37" (94 cm) in length.

YARN
Worsted weight (#4 Medium).

Shown here: Brown Sheep Lamb's Pride Superwash Worsted (100% wool; 200 yd [183 m]/100 g): #SW84 Shane's red (MC), 14 balls; #SW145 blaze (CC), 3 balls.

NEEDLES
Size 7 (4.5 mm): 24" (60 cm) circular (cir) and 2 double-pointed (dpn). Adjust needle size if necessary to obtain the correct gauge.

NOTIONS
Markers (m); stitch holders; cable needle (cn); tapestry needle.

GAUGE
21 stitches and 27 rows = 4" (10 cm) in stockinette stitch.

SUIKAN

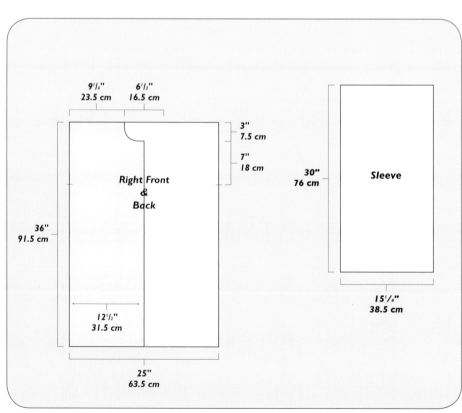

9¼"
23.5 cm

6½"
16.5 cm

3"
7.5 cm

7"
18 cm

30"
76 cm

Sleeve

Right Front
&
Back

36"
91.5 cm

12½"
31.5 cm

25"
63.5 cm

15¼"
38.5 cm

BACK

With MC and using the long-tail method (see Glossary, page 118), CO 130 sts. Purl 1 (WS) row. Cont in St st until piece measures 36" (91.5 cm) from CO, ending with a WS row. Place sts on holder.

RIGHT FRONT

With MC and using the long-tail method, CO 66 sts. Purl 1 (WS) row. Cont in St st until piece measures 33" (84 cm) from CO, ending with a WS row.

Shape Neck

At neck edge (beg of RS rows), BO 5 sts 1 time, then BO 3 sts 2 times, then BO 2 sts 2 times—51 sts rem. Dec 1 st at neck edge every RS row 3 times—48 sts rem. Cont even in St st until piece measures 36" (91.5 cm) from CO, ending with a WS row. Place sts on holder.

SUIKAN

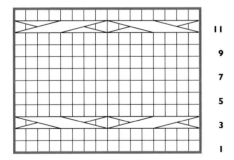

k on RS, p on WS

pattern repeat

4/4 RC: sl 4 sts onto cn and hold in back, k4, k4 from cn

4/4 LC: sl 4 sts onto cn and hold in front, k4, k4 from cn

LEFT FRONT

CO and work as for right front until piece measures 33" (84 cm), ending with a RS row.

Shape Neck

At neck edge (beg of WS rows), BO 5 sts 1 time, then BO 3 sts 2 times, then BO 2 sts 2 times—51 sts rem. Dec 1 st at neck edge every RS row 3 times—48 sts rem. Cont even in St st until piece measures 36" (91.5 cm) from CO, ending with a WS row. Place sts on holder.

RIGHT SLEEVE

Using the long-tail method, CO 3 sts with MC, 16 sts with CC, and 70 sts with MC—89 sts total. Using the intarsia method of twisting yarns around each other at color changes, purl 1 row in colors as established. *Next row:* (RS) Work all MC sts in St st and work CC sts according to Row 1 of Suikan chart. Cont in this manner, working MC sts in St st and CC sts as charted until piece measures about 30" (76 cm) from CO, ending with Row 12 of chart. BO all sts.

LEFT SLEEVE

Using the long-tail method, CO 70 sts with MC, 16 sts with CC, and 3 sts with MC—89 sts total. Work as for right sleeve.

FINISHING

Shoulder Seams

Place 130 back sts onto one needle and 48 right front sts onto another needle. With MC and RS tog, use the three-needle method (see Glossary, page 117) to BO 48 sts tog for right shoulder, BO next 34 back sts for back neck, then BO 48 left front sts tog with rem 48 back sts. Cut yarn, pull tail through rem st, and pull tight to secure.

Using the steam or wet-towel method (see Glossary, page 117), block pieces to measurements.

Right Front Okumi (overlap)

With CC and RS facing, pick up and knit 144 sts along right front edge to beg of neck shaping. Knit 1 (WS) row. Change to MC and knit 1 row. Beg with Row 2, work linen st (see Stitch Guide) for 3 rows. Work short-rows (see Glossary, page 124) as foll:

Short-Row 1: (RS) Work Row 1 of linen st to last 23 sts, wrap next st, turn, place marker (pm).

Short-Row 2: Sl 1 with yarn in back, work Row 2 of patt to end of row.

Short-Row 3: Work Row 1 of patt to 8 sts before m, wrap next st, turn, pm.

Short-Row 4: Rep Short-Row 2.

Rep the last 2 rows 10 more times—12 markers. Work Row 1 of patt, removing markers as you go (do not work wraps tog with wrapped sts). Work Row 2 of patt. *Next row:* BO all sts according to Row 1 of patt (k1, sl 1 with yarn in front, pass right st up and over left st to BO 1 st, k1, pass right st up and over left st to BO 1 st, sl 1 with yarn in front, pass right st up and over left st to BO, etc.).

Left Front Okumi

With CC, RS facing, and beg at neck shaping, pick up and knit 144 sts along left front edge. Knit 1 (WS) row. Change to MC and knit 1 row. Beg with Row 2, work linen st for 4 rows. Work short-rows as foll:

Short-Row 1: (WS) Work Row 2 of linen st to last 24 sts, wrap next st, turn, pm.

Short-Row 2: K1, sl 1 with yarn in front, work Row 1 of patt to end of row.

Short-Row 3: Work Row 2 of patt to 8 sts before m, wrap next st, turn, pm.

Short-Row 4: Rep Short-Row 2.

Rep the last 2 rows 10 more times—12 markers. Work Row 2 of patt, removing markers as you go (do not work wraps tog with wrapped sts). Work Row 1 of patt. *Next row:* BO all sts according to Row 2 of patt.

Collar

With CC, RS facing, and beg at right center front neck, pick up and knit 33 sts along front neck edge, 35 sts across back neck, and 33 along left front neck edge—101 sts total. Knit 1 (WS) row. Cont even in St st until piece measures 2" (5 cm) from pick-up row, ending with a WS row. With RS facing, BO all sts.

Side Seams

Mark 23" (58.5 cm) from lower edge on front and back at side edges. Match lower edges and marks and sew side seams from RS using MC and the mattress st with half-st seam allowance (see Glossary, page 123).

Hem

With CC, RS facing, and beg at left center front lower edge, pick up and knit 17 sts along linen st okumi, 65 sts across front to side seam, 129 sts across back, 65 sts across right front, and 17 sts along linen st okumi—293 sts total. Knit 1 (WS) row for garter ridge. Work even in St st until hem measures 2" (5 cm) from pick-up row, ending with a WS row. With RS facing, BO all sts. Allow hem to roll naturally.

Sleeve Seams

With MC threaded on a tapestry needle, match CO to BO edges and use an invisible horizontal seam (see Glossary, page 122) to sew sleeve seam, changing colors as necessary. Mark 10" (25.5 cm) down from shoulder on front and back at side edge. Mark mid-point on plain (not cable) selvedge edge of sleeve and match to shoulder seam. With MC,

RS facing, and using the mattress st, sew sleeves to body—lower 5" (12.5 cm) of sleeves will rem free.

Drawstring (make 2)

With MC and dpn, CO 4 sts. Work 4-st knit-cord (see Glossary, page 121) until piece measures 54" (137 cm) from CO. *Next row:* [K2tog] 2 times—2 sts rem. Pass right st over left st and off the needle. Cut yarn and pull tail through rem st to secure. Beg at lower edge of sleeve, insert knit cord behind each cable crossing. Even the ends and tie the ends tog in an overhand knot just below the bottom of the sleeve.

Knot Closure

With CC and dpn, CO 3 sts. Work 3-st knit-cord until piece measures 9½" (24 cm) for the loop side. Make a second knit-cord 11" (28 cm) long for the knot side. Tie a slipknot in the shorter piece so that the ends extend about 3" (7.5 cm) from the knot and the loop extends about 1" (2.5 cm) on the other side. Tie a Chinese knot into the longer piece, pulling until the knot is nice and round but not too snug—the ends should extend about 3" (7.5 cm) from the knot. Mark 2" (5 cm) down from the collar garter ridge on each front. Pin knot on St st portion of the left front and pin the loop on the St st portion of the right front so that the 3" (7.5 cm) extensions are perpendicular to the okumi garter ridge. With CC and WS facing, use a whipstitch (see Glossary, page 124) to sew in place.

Steam-block (see Glossary, page 117) to set seams, knot closure, okumi overlaps, and cable cuffs.

CHINESE KNOT

The Meiji Restoration (1868–1912) marked a return to understated

elegance following an era of colorful flamboyance and extravagance. This expression of style called iki emphasized muted colors and elaborate but barely visible woven patterns. Small-scale repeating patterns (komon) and fine stripes worked in dark shibui colors, such as subdued browns and off-greens, became favored. Decorative embroidery and dyed patterns were reserved for the interior lining of the kosode, where the wearer could privately enjoy a previously public aesthetic.

This kimono is knitted in one piece from cuff to cuff. The garter-stitch brick pattern provides a subtle allover texture reminiscent of the inconspicuous komon of the time; the spark of color in the facings captures the sense of understated elegance.

MATERIALS

FINISHED SIZE

About 50" (127 cm)—48" (122 cm) garment plus a 2" (2.5 cm) space at center front—and 42" (106.5 cm) in knitted length (will stretch to 46" [117 cm] front length at neckband and to 50" [127 cm] back length).

YARN

Worsted weight (#4 Medium).

Shown here: Blue Sky Alpacas Dyed Cotton (100% cotton; 150 yd [137 m]/100 g): #620 fern, 15 skeins; #619 tomato, 3 skeins; #622 pumpkin, 1 skein.

NEEDLES

Body and sleeves—size 10½ (6.5 mm): 32" (80 cm) circular (cir). Edging—size 8 (5 mm): 24" (60 cm) cir and two 32" (80 cm) or longer cir. Adjust needle size if necessary to obtain the correct gauge.

NOTIONS

Tapestry needle; K/10½ (6.5 mm) crochet hook; marker (m).

GAUGE

14 stitches and 22 rows = 4" (10 cm) in garter stitch brick pattern on larger needle; 16 stitches and 24 rows = 4" (10 cm) in stockinette stitch on smaller needle.

STITCH GUIDE

Garter Stitch Brick Pattern (multiple of 14 stitches)
Row 1: (WS) Knit.
Row 2 and all even-numbered rows: (RS) Knit.
Row 3: *K7, p7; rep from *.
Row 5: Knit.
Row 7: *P7, k7; rep from *.
Row 8: Knit.
Repeat Rows 1–8 for pattern.

NOTE

● The body and sleeves are made in a single piece from right cuff to left cuff.
The pattern stitch is worked at a looser gauge than the stockinette-stitch neckband so the body will be flexible and stretch while the neckband will remain stiffer and create the curved silhouette inherent in the design.

RIGHT SLEEVE

With larger needle and fern, CO 98 sts. Work Rows 1–8 of garter st brick patt (see Stitch Guide) 7 times, then work Rows 1–7 once more, ending with a WS row—piece measures about 11½" (29 cm) from CO.

FRONT AND BACK

With RS facing, use the cable method (see Glossary, page 118) to CO 98 sts for the right front, then knit across all sts according to Row 8 of patt. *Next row:* (WS) Use the cable method to CO 98 sts for the back (counts as Row 8 of patt)—294 sts total. Work Rows 1–8 of patt across all sts 6 times, then work Rows 1–3 once more—piece measures about 9½" (24 cm) from cable CO. *Next row:* (Row 4 of patt) With RS facing, BO 147 sts for right front edge, knit to end—147 sts rem. Keeping in patt, work Rows 5–8 once, then work Rows 1–8 two times, then work Rows 1–7 once—piece measures about 5" (12.5 cm) from front edge BO. *Next row:* (Row 8 of patt) With RS facing, use the cable method to CO 147 sts for left front edge, then knit across all sts—294 sts. Work Rows 1–8 of patt across all sts 6 times, then work Rows 1–3 once more—piece measures about 9½" (24 cm) from front edge CO. *Next row:* (Row 4 of patt) BO 98 sts for left front, knit to end—196 sts rem. *Next row:* (Row 5 of patt) BO 98 sts for back, work in patt to end—98 sts rem. Do not BO.

LEFT SLEEVE

Cont on 98 sts from front and back, work Rows 6–8 of patt once, then work Rows 1–8 seven times, then work Rows 1–3 once more—piece measures about 11½" (29 cm) from back BO. BO all sts.

FINISHING

Side and Sleeve Seams

Fold kimono at shoulders with RS tog. With fern and crochet hook, work a slip-stitch crochet seam (see Glossary, page 124) to join sides from hem to armhole, working stitch for stitch. With fern threaded on a tapestry needle, use the mattress stitch for garter stitch (see Glossary, page 123) to sew sleeve seams.

Hem Facing

With pumpkin, 24" (60 cm) smaller cir needle, and RS facing, pick up and knit 40 sts along lower left front edge, 100 stitches along lower back edge, and 40 sts along lower right front edge—180 sts total. Knit 1 row for garter ridge. Change to tomato and work even in St st until piece measures 2¼" (5.5 cm) from garter ridge. BO all sts. Fold facing to WS along garter ridge. With tomato threaded on a tapestry needle, use a whipstitch (see Glossary, page 124) to sew facing in place.

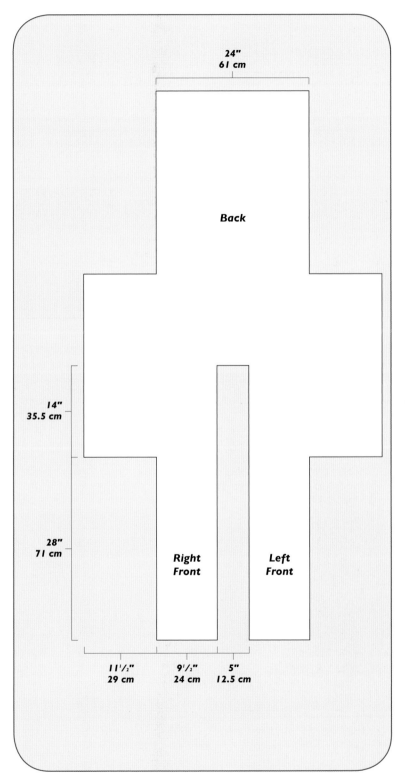

24"
61 cm

Back

14"
35.5 cm

28"
71 cm

Right Front

Left Front

11½"
29 cm

9½"
24 cm

5"
12.5 cm

Sleeve Facing

With pumpkin, 24" (60 cm) smaller cir needle, and RS facing, pick up and knit 98 sts around lower sleeve edge. Place marker (pm) and join for working in the rnd. Purl 1 rnd for garter ridge. Change to tomato and work even in St st until facing measures 1¾" (4.5 cm) from garter ridge. BO all sts. Fold facing to WS along garter ridge. Whipstitch in place.

Neckband

With pumpkin, first 32" (80 cm) smaller cir needle, and beg at lower center edge of right front, pick up and knit 1 st in pumpkin ridge, then 147 sts along right front to shoulder (pick up 1 st in each st), 20 sts across back neck, 147 sts along left front, and 1 st in other pumpkin ridge—316 sts total. With second 32" (80 cm) smaller needle, knit 1 row. Work with both circular needles to more easily accommodate all sts. Change to fern. Working the first 3 and last 3 sts in garter st, work rem sts in St st until piece measures 2¼" (5.5 cm) from garter ridge, ending with a RS row. Knit 1 WS row for garter ridge. Change to tomato and cont in St st with 3 st garter st edges for 2" (5 cm). BO all sts. Fold neckband facing to WS along fern garter ridge. Whipstitch in place.

Weave in loose ends.

Steam seams and press with fingers to compress seam allowance. Steam hem and sleeve facings. Lay garment out to measurements and lightly steam to block.

Dofuku were short jackets worn by samurai generals over

their armor on the battlefield or over kosode at home for relaxation. While a true kimono is a full-length garment, short kimono jackets abound in Japanese clothing. From the people's working kimono to short military battle jackets, they are made in everything from bast fibers to cotton to silk, and occasionally, imported woolens. As a basic wardrobe component, a short jacket is a hard worker for casual wear in a matte fiber, more formal in a luxurious fiber with sheen, and commanding in all black.

This very short kimono is knitted in stockinette stitch with a beaded rib at the lower edges and neckband. To wear closed, always overlap kimono left over right. (It is the opposite only for burial.) Although the fronts overlap, they may be worn hanging open. As a closure, use a short chopstick or hair adornment inserted in and out of the layers.

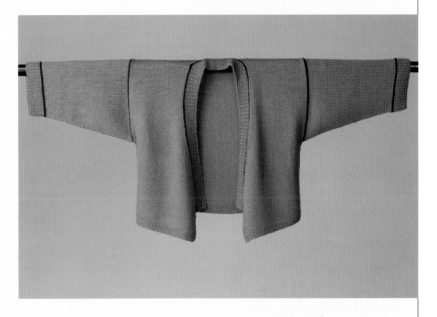

MATERIALS

FINISHED SIZE
About 44½ (48½)" (113 [123] cm) in circumference and 20 (22)" (51 [56] cm) in length.

YARN
Worsted weight (#4 Medium).
Shown here: Berroco Softwist (59% rayon, 41% wool; 100 yd [91 m]/ 50 g): #9439 ginger, 14 (16) skeins; #9434 pitch black, 1 skein

NEEDLES
Size 7 (4.5 mm): 24" (60 cm) circular (cir) and extra cir needle in same size for finishing. Adjust needle size if necessary to obtain the correct gauge.

NOTIONS
Stitch holders; tapestry needle; stick closure.

GAUGE
20 stitches and 28 rows = 4" (10 cm) in stockinette stitch.

BACK

With ginger, CO 111 (121) sts.

Row 1: (WS) *P1, k1; rep from * to last st, p1.

Row 2: (RS) Knit.

Rep Rows 1 and 2 three more times. Purl 1 (WS) row. Cont even in St st until piece measures 20 (22)" (51 [56] cm) from CO. Place sts on holder.

RIGHT FRONT

With ginger, CO 66 (70) sts.

Row 1: (WS) *P1, k1; rep from *.

Row 2: (RS) Knit.

Rep Rows 1 and 2 three more times. *Next row:* (WS) Purl to last 3 sts, k1, p1, k1. Knit 1 row. Rep the last 2 rows until piece measures 3 (5)" (7.5 [12.5] cm) from CO, ending with a WS row.

Shape Neck

(RS) K1, ssk, knit to end—1 st dec'd. Purl 1 row. Cont in St st, dec 1 st at beg of row in this manner every 4th row 25 more times—40 (44) sts rem. Cont even until piece measures 20 (22)" (51 [56] cm) from CO. Place sts on holder.

LEFT FRONT

With ginger, CO 66 (70) sts.

Row 1: (WS) *K1, p1, rep from *.

Row 2: Knit.

Rep Rows 1 and 2 three more times. *Next row:* (WS) K1, p1, k1, purl to

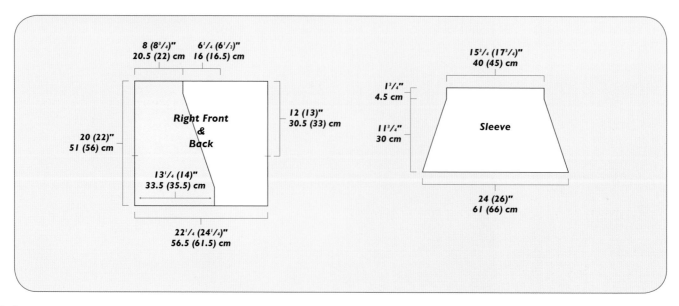

end. Knit 1 row. Rep the last 2 rows until piece measures 3 (5)" (7.5 [12.5] cm) from CO, ending with a WS row.

Shape Neck

(RS) Knit to last 3 sts, k2tog, k1—1 st dec'd. Purl 1 row. Cont in St st, dec 1 st at end of row in this manner every 4th row 25 more times—40 (44) sts rem. Cont even until piece measures 20 (22)" (51 [56] cm) from CO. Place sts on holder.

JOIN SHOULDERS

Place 111 (121) back sts onto one needle and 40 (44) right front sts on another needle. With ginger and RS tog, use the three-needle method (see Glossary, page 117) to BO 40 (44) right front and back sts tog for right shoulder, then BO next 31 (33) back sts for back neck, then BO rem 40 (44) back sts tog with 40 (44) left front sts for left shoulder. Cut yarn and pull tail through rem st to secure.

SLEEVES

Measure 12 (13)" (30.5 [33] cm) down from shoulder seam on front and back side edges and mark for sleeve placement. With black and RS facing, pick up and knit 120 (130) sts between markers. Knit 1 row. Change to ginger and work in St st, dec 1 st at each end of needle (i.e., k1, ssk, knit to last 3 sts, k2tog, k1) every 4th row 20 times, ending with a WS row—80 (90) sts rem.

Cuff

Change to black and knit 1 row, dec 1 st—79 (89) sts rem. Knit 1 (WS) row for garter ridge. Change to ginger and work as foll:

Row 1: (RS) Knit.

Row 2: *P1, k1; rep from * to last st, p1.

Rep Rows 1 and 2 until cuff measures 1¾" (4.5 cm) from black garter ridge, ending with a RS row. With WS facing, BO all sts in patt.

FINISHING

Front Neckband

With black, RS facing, and beg at right center front at beg of decreases 3 (5)" (7.5 [12.5] cm) above CO edge, pick up and knit 87 sts along right front edge, 31 (33) sts across back neck, and 87 sts along left front edge to point 3 (5)" (7.5 [12.5] cm) above CO edge on left front—205 (207) sts total. Knit 1 (WS) row for garter ridge. Change to ginger and work as foll:

Row 1: (RS) Knit.

Row 2: *K1, p1; rep from * to last st, k1.

Rep Rows 1 and 2 until neckband measures 2" (5 cm) from black garter ridge, ending with a RS row. With WS facing, BO all sts in patt.

Seams

With ginger threaded on a tapestry needle, use the mattress st with ½-st seam allowance (see Glossary, page 123) to sew side and sleeve seams. Weave in loose ends. Block, using the wet-towel method (see Glossary, page 117).

Komon are small, textural pattern repeats worked in a single

color or small-scale stencil-resist designs (an incredibly labor-intensive process) worked in subdued colors. When viewed as an overall solid, kimono made with komon fabrics are visions of restrained elegance. As a response to Meiji governmental restraints on flamboyantly bright colors and exuberant textile design, emphasis was placed on beautiful subtle variations. This aesthetic was appreciated by all classes from elite to common. Komon included an endless variety of patterns including narrow stripes, wide stripes, wide and narrow stripes, arrow stripes, triple stripes, even squares, uneven rectangles, repeating diamonds, plaids, and lattices.

In this knitted version, I have used yarnover stitches to create a small textural pattern that emulates latticework. The sleeves are comparatively shallow and the front opening falls straight from the shoulders. The deep red—dyes traditionally reserved for nobility—and the pressed sheen and beautiful drape of the rayon ribbon give an attitude of formality to this short kimono, called *haori*.

MATERIALS

FINISHED SIZE
About 44½" (113 cm) in circumference—43¼" (110 cm) garment plus a 1¼" (3.2 cm) space at center front—and 28" (71 cm) in length.

YARN
Worsted weight (#4 Medium).
Shown here: Berroco Glacé (100% rayon; 75 yd [69 m]/50 g): #2560 maddar lake, 20 skeins.

NEEDLES
Body and sleeves—size 9 (5.5 mm): 24" (60 cm) circular (cir); neckband—size 6 (4 mm): straight or cir. Adjust needle size if necessary to obtain the correct gauge.

NOTIONS
Size G/6 (4 mm) crochet hook; open-ring markers (m); tapestry needle; knitter's pins.

GAUGE
15 stitches and 16 rows = 4" (10 cm) in pattern stitch on larger needle.

KOMON

STITCH GUIDE

Pattern Stitch (multiple of 2 stitches + 1)

Row 1: (RS) K1, *yo, k2; rep from
*—1 st inc'd per patt rep.

Row 2: (WS) P1, *p3, pass the first st
of the 3 over the other 2 and off the
needle; rep from *—1 st dec'd per
patt rep.

Row 3: *K2, yo; rep from * to last st,
k1—1 st inc'd per patt rep.

Row 4: *P3, pass the first st of the 3 over
the other 2 and off the needle; rep
from * to last st, p1—1 st dec'd per patt rep.

Repeat Rows 1–4 for pattern.

NOTE

● When winding this yarn into a ball, it is helpful to wrap a rubber band around the ball
once or twice during the process. Doing this, and working from the outside of the ball, will

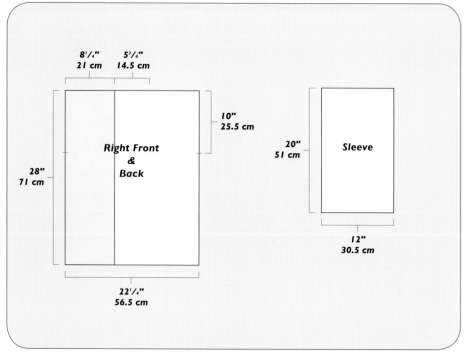

BACK

With larger needle, CO 83 sts. Purl 1 (WS) row. Rep Rows 1–4 of patt st (see Stitch Guide) until piece measures 28" (71 cm) from CO, ending with a WS row. BO all sts.

FRONT (make 2)

With larger needle, CO 31 sts. Purl 1 (WS) row. Rep Rows 1–4 of patt st until piece measures 28" (71 cm) from CO, ending with a WS row. BO all sts.

SLEEVES

With larger needle, CO 45 sts. Purl 1 (WS) row. Rep Rows 1–4 of patt st until piece measures 20" (51 cm) from CO, ending with a WS row. BO all sts.

FINISHING

Join Shoulders

With RS tog and side edges aligned, use slip-stitch crochet (see Glossary, page 124) to join fronts to back at shoulders.

Sleeve Seams

Fold sleeve with RS tog so that CO and BO edges meet. Join CO to BO edge using slip-stitch crochet. With iron set for rayon, firmly press seams. Mark 10" (25.5 cm) down from shoulder on front and back at side edges. With larger needle and RS facing, pick up and knit 100 sts between markers. With WS facing, BO all sts kwise for garter ridge on RS. Mark mid-point of sleeve and match to shoulder seam. Sew sleeve to garter edging using the mattress st with ½-st seam allowance (see Glossary, page 123).

Neckband

With smaller needle, CO 14 sts.

Row 1: K11, sl 3 sts pwise with yarn in front.

Row 2: Knit.

Rep Rows 1 and 2 until piece measures 56" (142 cm) from CO, ending with Row 1. Leave sts on needle; do not cut yarn. Pin band in place, starting at lower edge of front, stretching band slightly to prevent sagging, and keeping knitted cord (slipped sts) at outside edge. Beg at lower front edge, use the mattress st to sew band up one front, across back neck, and down other front. If necessary, add or subtract rows in the band for an exact fit, ending with Row 1 of patt. To finish, knit the first 2 sl sts tog, then work the remainder of the row as a normal BO. Sew rem band in place. Weave in loose ends.

With iron set to rayon, press entire kimono to compress yarn and create drape.

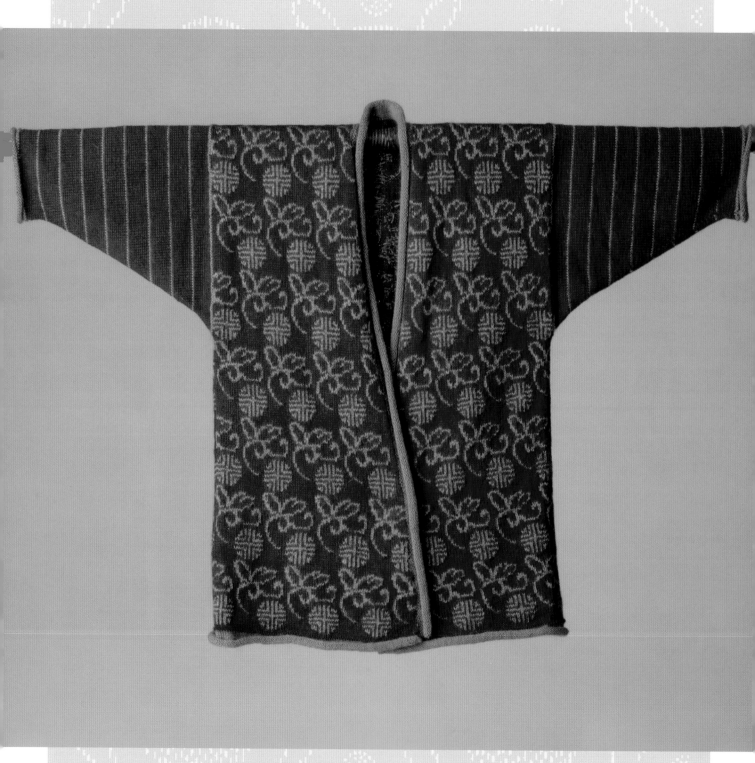

Medallions & Scrolls

During the Kamakura period (1185–1333), extremely skilled

artisans wove rich brocade fabrics featuring small repeating patterns. Men of the warrior class wore an ensemble called a hitatare made of this fabric. A kimono-like top with cropped trousers, a hitatare was worn under armor during battle and as public wear at other times. In the succeeding Muromachi age (1333–1573), the patterns evolved into more flamboyant large-scale decorative patterns called *daimon*. The practical Kamakura hitatare warrior suits became ceremonial garb for daimyo regional lords in the Edo period (1600–1867).

I have taken the middle road between small and large scale, working with medallions and scrolling leaf images to give an impression of sophisticated elegance. The standard kimono shape is modified with overlapping fronts and shaped sleeves. A spark of contrasting color peeks out at front and sleeve edges that may be stitched as a hem or left as a roll at the bottom edge. Although wool had not been widely used in Japan, woolens were imported during the early Meiji years (1868–1912).

MATERIALS

FINISHED SIZE
About 52" (132 cm) in circumference and 33" (84 cm) in length.

YARN
Sportweight (#2 Fine).
Shown here: Dalegarn Tiur (60% mohair, 40% pure new wool; 126 yd [115 m]/50 g): #4155 dark wine (MC), 14 balls; #9853 olive (CC), 8 balls.

NEEDLES
Size 4 (3.5 mm): two 32" (80 cm) circular (cir). Adjust needle size if necessary to obtain the correct gauge.

NOTIONS
Open-ring markers; stitch holders; tapestry needle.

GAUGE
24 stitches and 28 rows = 4" (10 cm) in charted pattern.

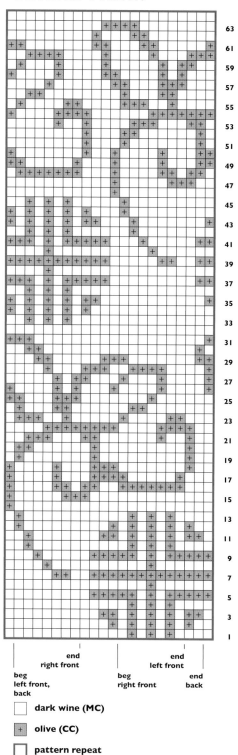

63
61
59
57
55
53
51
49
47
45
43
41
39
37
35
33
31
29
27
25
23
21
19
17
15
13
11
9
7
5
3
1

end
right front

end
left front

beg
left front,
back

beg
right front

end
back

☐ dark wine (MC)

⊞ olive (CC)

☐ pattern repeat

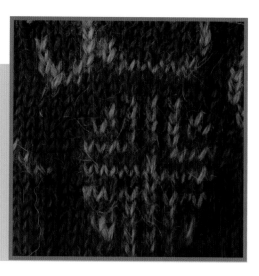

NOTE

● The motifs are worked in a combination of Fair Isle and intarsia techniques, with unused colors stranded across the back only when necessary.

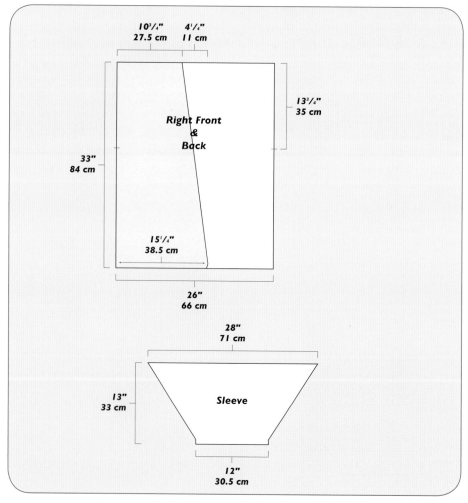

10³/₄"
27.5 cm

4¹/₄"
11 cm

13³/₄"
35 cm

Right Front
&
Back

33"
84 cm

15¹/₄"
38.5 cm

26"
66 cm

28"
71 cm

13"
33 cm

Sleeve

12"
30.5 cm

BACK

With CC, CO 156 sts. Work in St st until piece measures 2" (5 cm) from CO, ending with a WS row. Change to MC and knit 2 rows for garter ridge, then work 2 rows in St st. Work Rows 1–64 of Medallions and Scrolls chart 2 times, beg and ending as indicated for back—128 rows. Mark each side edge for underarm. Work Rows 1–64, then work Rows 1–32 once more—224 rows total. Place sts on holder.

LEFT FRONT

With CC, CO 90 sts. Work in St st, inc 1 st at end of a RS row when piece measures 1" (2.5 cm) from CO, and again when piece measures 2" (5 cm) from CO, ending with a WS row—92 sts. Change to MC and knit 2 rows for garter ridge, then work 2 rows in St st. Work Rows 1–64 two times, beg and ending as indicated for left front, then mark side edge (beg of RS row) for underarm, then work Rows 1–64 once, then work Rows 1–32 once more—224 rows total, and *at the same time* dec 1 st at center front (end of RS rows) every 8th row 27 times—65 sts rem. Place all sts on holder.

RIGHT FRONT

With CC, CO 90 sts. Work in St st, inc 1 st at beg of a RS row when work measures 1" (2.5 cm) from CO, and then again at 2" (5 cm) from CO, ending with a WS row—92 sts. Change to MC and knit 2 rows for garter ridge, then work 2 rows in St st. Work Rows 1–64 two times, beg and ending as indicated for right front, then mark side edge (end of RS row) for underarm, then work Rows 1–64 once, then work Rows 1–32 once more—224 rows total, and *at the same time* dec 1 st at center front (beg of RS rows) every 8th row 27 times—65 sts rem. Place all sts on holder.

SHOULDER SEAMS

Place 156 back sts onto one needle and 65 right front sts onto another needle. With RS tog, use the three-needle method (see Glossary, page 117) to BO 65 sts tog for right shoulder, BO next 26 back sts for back neck, then BO next 65 back sts tog with 65 left front sts for left shoulder. Cut yarn and pull tail through rem st to secure.

SLEEVES

With CC and RS facing, pick up and knit 168 sts between underarm markers on side edge of front and back. Knit 1 (WS) row. Working in St st, work stripes as foll: [10 rows MC, 1 row CC] 8 times, then work

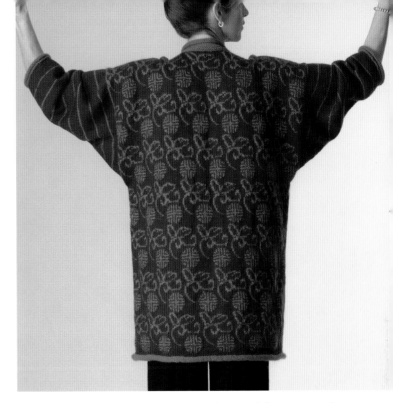

10 rows MC, and *at the same time* shape sleeve as foll: BO 2 sts at beg of every row 8 times—152 sts rem. **Next row:** (RS) K1, k2tog, knit to last 3 sts, ssk, k1—2 sts dec'd. Dec 1 st each end of needle in this manner every RS row 39 more times—72 sts rem; piece measures about 12½" (31.5 cm) after final 10 rows of MC have been worked. Change to CC and knit 2 rows for garter ridge, then cont in St st until piece measures 1" (2.5 cm) from garter ridge. BO all sts.

FINISHING

Neckband

With CC, RS facing, and beg at right center front lower edge, pick up and knit 172 sts along right front, 27 sts across back neck, and 172 sts along left front—371 sts total. Using second needle (to knit all sts back and forth from one needle to the other), knit 3 rows (2 garter ridges on RS). Cont even in St st until piece measures 2" (5 cm) from last garter ridge. Loosely BO all sts.

Side and Sleeve Seams

With MC threaded on a tapestry needle, use the mattress st (see Glossary, page 123) to sew side and sleeve seams.

Using the wet-towel method (see Glossary, page 117), block to measurements. If desired, press on WS to flatten some of the motif thickness.

Haori with Crests

A wafuku jacket, or haori, is a shorter version of kimono that

originated for males. The most formal of this type of kimono is the unpatterned monochrome kimono *(iro muji)* with one, three, or five crests. The Japanese crest (mon) is a stylized motif, usually defined by a circle, that combines messages of heraldry, logo, and sheer design. Crests have a multilayered history, rich with extensive definition for family, samurai, and nobility. The presence or absence of crests is the clearest mark of formality. While there may be formal kimono without crests, there are no informal kimono with crests. Around 1895, female commoners began to wear black crepe haori with crests for high ceremonial wear. By the early twentieth century, different colored and patterned haori came into vogue and were used much like a Westerner would put on a jacket to finish and formalize an ensemble.

The exquisite hand of the bamboo fiber in this knitted version lends itself well to the formal type of kimono. The slight sheen to the fiber, the smooth stockinette stitch texture, and the beautiful drape of the knitted fabric combine to provide an elegant look and feel. With the embroidered crests, this kimono pays admirable homage to the haori.

MATERIALS

FINISHED SIZE
About 51½" (131 cm) in circumference—50¼" (127.5 cm) garment plus a 1¼" (3.2 cm) space at center front—and 34" (86.5 cm) in length (stretches to 40" [101.5 cm]).

YARN
Worsted weight (#4 Medium).
Shown here: Plymouth Royal Bamboo (100% bamboo; 93 yd [85 m]/50 g): #58 dark plum (MC), 26 balls; #02 light ochre (CC), 1 ball.

NEEDLES
Size 8 (5 mm): 24" (60 cm) circular (cir); spare needle the same size or smaller for three-needle bind-off. Adjust needle size if necessary to obtain the correct gauge.

NOTIONS
Stitch holders or waste yarn; markers (m); tapestry needle; size H/8 (5 mm) crochet hook; knitter's pins.

GAUGE
20 stitches and 26 rows = 4" (10 cm) in stockinette stitch.

STITCH GUIDE

Bamboo Rib Pattern
(multiple of 4 stitches)

Rows 1 and 3: (RS) K1, *p2, k2; rep from * to last 3 sts, p2, k1.

Row 2: P1, k1, *skip next 3 sts and insert needle into front of fourth st and draw a loop through, then knit first st on left-hand needle, purl next 2 sts on left-hand needle, then drop the original fourth st off needle (this st has already been knitted with the long loop); rep from * to last 2 sts, k1, p1.

Row 4: P1, *k2, p2; rep from * to last 3 sts, k2, p1.
Repeat Rows 1–4 for pattern.

NOTE

● To ensure a smooth finished front border edge, join new balls of yarn at the side seam edge, rather than the front border edge or in the middle of the work.

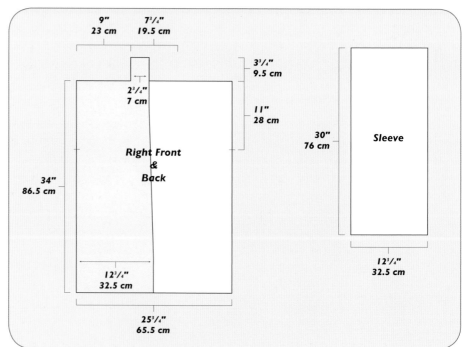

BACK

With MC and using the long-tail method (see Glossary, page 118), CO 172 sts. Purl 1 row. Work Rows 1–4 of bamboo rib patt (see Stitch Guide) 2 times, then work Rows 1 and 2 once more. *Dec row:* (RS) K1, *k2tog, k2; rep from * to last 3 sts, k2tog, k1—129 sts rem. Work even in St st until piece measures 34" (86.5 cm) from CO. Place sts on holder.

RIGHT FRONT

With MC and using the long-tail method, CO 88 sts. Purl 1 row. Work in bamboo rib patt, but work first st on RS rows as sl 1 purlwise with yarn in back (pwise wyb) instead of k1. Work Rows 1–4 two times, then work Rows 1 and 2 once more. *Next row:* (RS) Cont in patt, work 20 sts, place marker (pm), dec 18 sts in rem 68 sts as foll: k2, [k1, k2tog, k2, k2tog] 9 times, k3—70 sts rem; 20 sts before m, 50 sts after m. Slip marker (sl m) every row. Work 50 sts after m in St st and 20 sts before m in bamboo rib until piece measures 6" (15 cm) from CO, ending with a WS row. *Next row:* (RS) Work 20 sts in rib patt, sl m, k1, k2tog, knit to end—69 sts rem; 20 sts before m, 49 sts after m. Cont in patt as established, dec 1 st after m in this manner every 6" (15 cm) 4 more times—65 sts rem; 20 sts before m, 45 sts after m. Work even until piece measures 34" (86.5 cm) from CO. Place 20 sts of bamboo rib on one holder; place rem 45 sts on a second holder.

LEFT FRONT

With MC and using the long-tail method, CO 88 sts. Purl 1 row. Work in bamboo rib patt, but work first st on WS rows as sl 1 pwise with yarn in front (wyf) instead of p1. Work Rows 1–4 two times, then work Rows 1 and 2 once more. *Next row:* (RS) Dec 18 sts in first 68 sts as foll: k2, [k1, k2tog, k2, k2tog] 9 times, k3, pm, work rem 20 sts in bamboo rib patt as established—70 sts rem; 50 sts before m, 20 sts after m. Work even as established until piece measures 6" (15 cm) from CO, ending with a WS row. *Next row:* (RS) Knit to 3 sts before m, ssk, k1, sl m, work to end in rib patt—69 sts rem; 49 sts before m, 20 sts after m. Cont even in patt as established, dec 1 st before m in this manner every 6" (15 cm) 4 more times—65 sts rem; 45 sts before m, 20 sts after m. Work even until piece measures 34" (86.5 cm) from CO. Place 20 sts of bamboo rib on one holder; place rem 45 sts on another holder.

LEFT SLEEVE

With MC and using the long-tail method, CO 67 sts. Purl 1 row.

Rows 1 and 3: (RS) Sl 1 pwise wyb, [p2, k2] 2 times, p2, k1, pm, k47, pm, k1, p2, k2, p2, k1.

Row 2: P1, k1, skip next 3 sts and insert needle into front of fourth st and draw a loop through, knit first st on left-hand needle, purl next 2 sts on left-hand needle, then drop the original fourth st off needle, k1, p1, sl m, p47, sl m, p1, k1, [skip next 3 sts and insert needle into front of fourth st and draw a loop through, knit first st on left-hand needle, purl next 2 sts on left-hand needle, then drop the original fourth st off needle] 2 times, k1, p1.

Row 4: P1, k2, p2, k2, p1, sl m, p47, sl m, p1, [k2, p2] 2 times, k2, p1.

Rep Rows 1–4 until piece measures 30" (76 cm) from CO, ending with Row 3. *Next row:* (Row 4) BO all sts in patt. Pull entire ball through last loop to secure. Fold sleeve in half with RS tog, matching CO and BO edges. With attached yarn and crochet hook, use slip-stitch crochet (see Glossary, page 124) to seam CO edge to BO edge.

RIGHT SLEEVE

With MC and using the long-tail method, CO 67 sts. Purl 1 row.

Rows 1 and 3: (RS) K1, p2, k2, p2, k1, pm, k47, pm, k1, [p2, k2] 2 times, p2, k1.

Row 2: Sl 1 pwise wyf, [k1, skip next 3 sts and insert needle into front of fourth st and draw a loop through, knit first st on left-hand needle, purl next 2 sts on left-hand needle, then drop the original fourth st off needle] 2 times, k1, p1, sl m, p47, sl m, p1, k1, skip next 3 sts and insert needle into front of fourth st and draw a loop through, knit first st on left-hand needle, purl next 2 sts on left-hand needle, then drop the original fourth st off needle, k1, p1.

Row 4: Sl 1 pwise wyf, [k2, p2] 2 times, k2, p1, sl m, p47, sl m, p1, k2, p2, k2, p1.

Rep Rows 1–4 until piece measures 30" (76 cm) from CO, ending with Row 3. *Next row:* (Row 4) BO all sts in patt. Pull entire ball through last loop to secure. Fold sleeve in half with RS tog, matching CO and BO edges. With attached yarn and crochet hook, use slip-stitch crochet to seam CO edge to BO edge.

FINISHING

Join Shoulders

Place 129 back sts onto one needle and 45 right front sts onto another needle. With RS tog, use the three-needle method (see Glossary, page 117) to BO 45 right front sts tog with 45 back sts for right shoulder, BO 39 sts of back for back neck, then place 45 held left front sts onto a

spare needle and use the three-needle method to BO 45 left front sts tog with rem 45 back sts for left shoulder.

Neckband

Left front border: Place 20 held sts of left front border (bamboo rib sts) onto needle and cont in patt until piece measures about 3¾" (9.5 cm) from shoulder seam, ending with Row 3 of patt. Cut yarn, leaving a 24" (61 cm) tail. Place sts on holder.

Right front border: Work as for left front border.

Hold the left front border and right front border with WS tog, with left front behind right front, and needles parallel. With tail from left front border threaded on a tapestry needle and working from the finished edge toward the back neck edge of border, graft the two borders tog at the center back as foll (this graft is ½ st off due to the knitting coming from opposite directions, but is still a nearly invisible join):

Step 1: Insert tapestry needle into first stitch on front needle (right front) pwise and leave this st on needle, insert tapestry needle into first st on back needle (left front) kwise and leave this st on the needle.

Step 2: Insert tapestry needle into first st on front needle kwise and drop this st off the needle, insert tapestry needle into next st kwise and leave this st on the needle.

Step 3: Insert tapestry needle into first st on back needle pwise and drop this st off the needle, insert tapestry needle into next st pwise and leave this st on the needle.

Step 4: Insert tapestry needle into first st on front needle pwise and drop this st off the needle, insert tapestry needle into next st kwise and leave this st on the needle.

Step 5: Insert tapestry needle into first st on back needle kwise and drop this st off the needle, insert tapestry needle into next st pwise and leave this st on the needle.

Step 6: Insert tapestry needle into first st on front needle pwise and drop this st off the needle, insert tapestry needle into next st pwise and leave this st on the needle.

Step 7: Insert tapestry needle into first st on back needle kwise and drop this st off the needle, insert tapestry needle into next st kwise and leave this st on the needle.

Step 8: Insert tapestry needle into first st on front needle kwise and drop this st off the needle, insert tapestry needle into next st pwise and leave this st on the needle.

Step 9: Insert tapestry needle into first st on back needle pwise and drop this st off the needle, insert tapestry needle into next st kwise and leave this st on the needle.

Step 10: Insert tapestry needle into first st on front needle kwise and drop this st off the needle, insert tapestry needle into next st kwise and leave this st on the needle.

Step 11: Insert tapestry needle into first st on back needle pwise and drop this st off the needle, insert tapestry needle into next st pwise and leave this st on the needle.

Step 12: Insert tapestry needle into first st on front needle pwise and drop this st off the needle, insert tapestry needle into next st kwise and leave this st on the needle.

Step 13: Insert tapestry needle into first st on back needle kwise and drop this st off the needle, insert tapestry needle into next st pwise and leave this st on the needle.

Steps 14–37: Repeat Steps 6–13 three more times.

Step 38: Insert tapestry needle into first st on front needle pwise and drop this st off the needle, insert tapestry needle into next st pwise and drop this st off the needle.

Step 39: Insert tapestry needle into first st on back needle kwise and drop this st off the needle, insert tapestry needle into next st kwise and drop this st off the needle.

Pin neckband to back neck and with MC threaded on a tapestry needle and RS facing, use the mattress stitch (see Glossary, page 123) to sew in place.

Side and Sleeve Seams

Mark 11" (28 cm) down from shoulder seam on front and back at side edges. Pin fronts to back along side seams. Use the mattress stitch to sew side seams from lower edge to marker. Mark 10" (25.5 cm) down from shoulder on front and back at side edges. Matching midpoint of sleeve to shoulder seam and keeping 2 reps of bamboo rib at cuff edge, use the mattress stitch to sew sleeve into armhole. Sleeve is not joined below the 10" (25.5 cm) mark.

Embroidery

With CC, tapestry needle, and following the illustration at right, use a stem stitch (see Glossary, page 120) to embroider 5 crests on garment, placing one at the center back about 2¼" (5.5 cm) below back neck, one each on right front and left front about 2¼" (5.5 cm) below shoulder seam (centered on each front), and one on the back of each sleeve about 2" (5 cm) below fold at top of sleeve (centered along length of sleeve). Block to measurements (blocking helps gives the fabric a more fluid look).

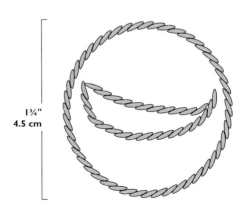

1¾"
4.5 cm

〰〰〰 **stem stitch, light ochre**

Fan Kimono

Hitoe, similar to the older term *katabira*, is an unlined robe.

In modern terms, it is reserved for the summer months and is made of cotton or silk. Kimono fabric and design is regulated by the months and seasons, temperature, designs and patterns that have seasonal connotations, and colors that reflect specific times of the year. For example, in the autumn month of October, an unlined kimono could be worn but only if it had darker, richer colors than one worn in the middle of summer.

This cotton kimono is of the short haori jacket variety, in a light terra-cotta color considered appropriate for summer months. The lacy stitch pattern resembles a fan shape, a common theme in feminine kimono. The body of this kimono is worked in a single piece from the back lower edge, up over the shoulders, and down the front, with stitches cast on and bound off for the sleeves along the way. This type of construction allows the fan stitch pattern to flow continuously over the entire garment. The neckband and sleeve edges are added at the end.

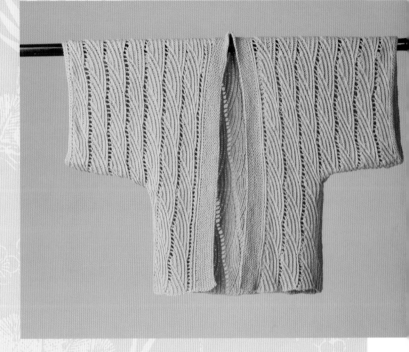

MATERIALS

FINISHED SIZE
About 49½" (125.5 cm) in circumference—47¾" (121.5 cm) garment plus a 1¾" (4.5 cm) space at center front—and 30½" (77.5 cm) in length.

YARN
Worsted weight (#4 Medium).
Shown here: Plymouth Fantasy Naturale (100% cotton; 140 yd [128 m]/100 g): #7250 orange, 10 skeins.

NEEDLES
Size 10 (6 mm): 24" (60 cm) circular (cir). Adjust needle size if necessary to obtain the correct gauge.

NOTIONS
16 markers (m); knitter's pins; tapestry needle; size J/10 (6 mm) crochet hook.

GAUGE
15 stitches and 16½ rows = 4" (10 cm) in fan stitch, after blocking.

FAN KIMONO

NOTE

● Place a marker after each chart repeat to make it easier to keep your place.

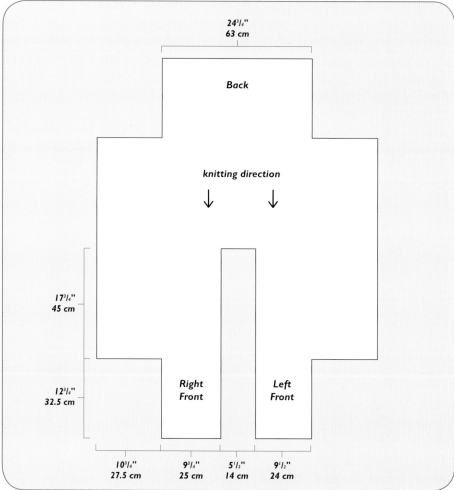

24³/₄"
63 cm

Back

knitting direction

↓   ↓

17³/₄"
45 cm

12³/₄"
32.5 cm

Right
Front

Left
Front

10³/₄"
27.5 cm

9³/₄"
25 cm

5¹/₂"
14 cm

9¹/₂"
24 cm

BACK

CO 93 sts. Purl 1 (WS) row. *Next row:* K1 (selvedge st; work in St st), k1 through back loop (tbl); work 90 sts according to Fan chart, k1 (selvedge st; work in St st). Work Rows 1–18 of chart 2 times, then work Rows 1–17 once more—piece measures about 12¾" (32.5 cm) from CO.

Cast On for Sleeves

With WS facing and using the cable method (see Glossary, page 118), CO 40 sts for left sleeve—133 sts. With WS still facing, purl these 40 sts, p1 through back loop (p1tbl), work next 90 sts according to Row 18 of chart, p1tbl, p1. *Next row:* With RS facing, use the cable method to CO 40 sts for right sleeve—173 sts total. With RS still facing, k1 (selvedge st), k1tbl, work Row 1 of chart to last st, k1 (selvedge st). Cont as established through Row 18 of chart, then work Rows 1–18 three more times—piece measures about 30½" (77.5 cm) from CO.

Shape Neck

(RS) Work 77 sts in patt, BO 21 sts in patt for neck (not working any additional yarnovers), work in patt to end of row—77 sts rem for right front/sleeve and 75 sts rem for left front/sleeve.

Left Sleeve and Front

With WS facing, work 75 left sleeve and front sts as foll: p1 (selvedge st), work 70 sts in patt (Row 2 of chart), place marker (pm), p1tbl, k1, p1tbl, p1. *Next row:* (RS, Row 3 of chart) K1, k1tbl, p1, k1tbl, work as charted to last st, k1 (selvedge st). Cont as established, working rib at center front edge and selvedge st at cuff edge, work Rows 4–18 of chart once, then work Rows 1–18 two more times, then work Rows 1–17 once more. *Next row:* (Row 18 of chart) Keeping in patt, BO 40 sts for left sleeve, work to end—35 sts rem. *Next row:* (Row 1 of chart) K1, k1tbl, p1, k1tbl, work as charted to last st, k1 (selvedge st). Cont as established, work Rows 2–18, then work Rows 1–18 two more times—piece measures 30½" (77.5 cm) from neck BO. BO all sts in patt.

Right Sleeve and Front

With WS facing, join yarn to 77 right front and sleeve sts. *Next row:* (WS) P1, p1tbl, k1, p1tbl, p1, pm, work as charted to last 2 sts, p1tbl, p1 (selvedge st). *Next row:* (RS) K1, k1tbl, work as charted to m, sl m, yo, k2tog tbl, p1, k1tbl, k1. Rep the last 2 rows, working Rows 4–18 once, then working Rows 1–18 three more times. *Next row:* (RS) Cont in patt, BO 40 sts for right sleeve, work to end—37 sts rem. *Next row:* (WS) P1, p1tbl, k1, p1tbl, p1, sl m, work as charted to last 2 sts, p1tbl, p1 (selvedge st). Cont as established, work Rows 3–18 of chart once, then work Rows 1–18 two more times—piece measures 30½" (77.5 cm) from neck BO. BO all sts in patt.

FAN

```
b • b • b • b • b
\ • b • b • b • b • b O   17
b b • b • b • b •
b \ • b • b • b • O        15
b • b • b • b • b
b • \ • b • b • b O        13
b • b • b • b • b
b • b \ • b • b • O        11
b • b • b • b • b
b • b • \ • b • b O         9
b • b • b • b • b
b • b • b \ • b • O         7
b • b • b • b • b
b • b • b • \ • b O         5
b • b • b • b b •
b • b • b • b \ • O         3
b • b • b • b • b
b • b • b • b • \           1
```

Legend:

☐	k on RS, p on WS
•	p on RS, k on WS
b	k tbl on RS, p tbl on WS
o	yo
\	k2tog tbl
☐	pattern repeat

FINISHING

Block piece to measurements using the wet-towel method (see Glossary, page 117).

Side and Sleeve Seams

Fold kimono at shoulder line with WS tog. Matching lower edges and underarms, pin side seams. With yarn threaded on a tapestry needle, RS facing, and using the mattress st with ½ stitch seam allowance (see Glossary, page 123), sew side seams. Turn garment WS out and pin sleeve seams. With crochet hook, use slip-stitch crochet (see Glossary, page 124) to join sleeve seams.

Steam seams to flatten and set.

Neckband

With RS facing, pick up and knit 91 sts along right front edge, 15 sts across back neck, and 91 sts along left front edge (pick up about 3 sts for every 4 rows along right and left front edges, and about 2 sts for every 3 sts across back neck edge)—197 sts total. Knit 1 (WS) row. *Next row:* Sl 1, knit to end. Rep the last row until neckband measures 2" (5 cm) from pick-up row, ending with a RS row. With WS facing, loosely BO all sts kwise.

Sleeve Border

With RS facing, pick up and knit about 103 sts along sleeve cuff (about 3 sts for every 4 rows). Pm and join for working in the rnd. Purl 1 rnd. BO all sts pwise.

Noh drama emerged in its present form in the late fourteenth

century. It has inauspicious roots as an agricultural festival, complete with singing and dancing and everyday clothing for costumes. Noh reached highly refined artistic heights in the Edo period (1600–1867) under the patronage of the Tokugawa shoguns who spared no expense in staging magnificent performances. While grand and dramatic, Noh is also poetic and formal, requiring special robes for the setting and storytelling. Costumes became formalized and extremely luxurious. Stage kosode were made of only the finest materials: heavily embroidered silks, fabric imprinted with gold and silver leaf, and sumptuous brocades (nishiki). Textile artists for Noh theater combined themes from nature and used geometric shapes with extraordinary sensitivity, at times bold and at others delicate.

To capture the luscious flavor of brocade without the stiffness, I chose a cotton yarn with a bit of sheen and supple drape for an overall look of muted opulence. I worked the fronts and back from the top down on the bias to create bold diagonal stripes. As a final touch, I added a bit of embroidery on the sleeves that suggests a floral motif and softens the strong angular pattern.

MATERIALS

FINISHED SIZE
About 53" (134.5 cm) in circumference—50½" (128.5 cm) garment plus a 2½" (6.5 cm) space at center front—and 41" (104 cm) in length.

YARN
Worsted weight (#4 Medium).

Shown here: Berroco Cotton Twist (70% mercerized cotton, 30% rayon; 85 yd [78 m]/50 g): #8464 morandi mix (multicolored; MC), 12 skeins; #8345 sensei (orange, CC1), 8 skeins; #8387 soul (dark plum, CC2), 5 skeins; #8322 fern (olive, CC3) and #8383 cork (yellow, CC4), 3 skeins each.

NEEDLES
Body and sleeves—size 9 (5.5 mm): 24" (60 cm) circular (cir); neckband —size 7 (4.5 mm). Adjust needle size if necessary to obtain the correct gauge.

NOTIONS
Markers (m); stitch holder; size G/6 (4 mm) crochet hook; tapestry needle; knitters' pins.

GAUGE
17 stitches and 25 rows = 4" (10 cm) in stockinette stitch on larger needle.

BOLD CHEVRON

NOTE

● The fronts and back are worked from the top down on the bias.

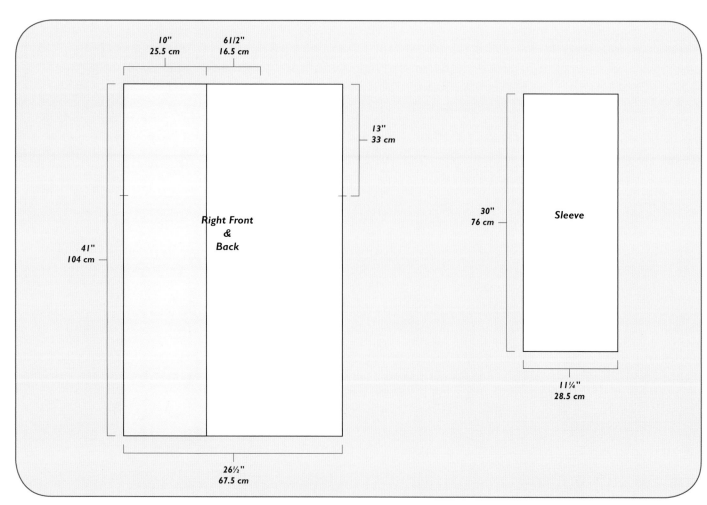

10"
25.5 cm

6½"
16.5 cm

13"
33 cm

Right Front
&
Back

41"
104 cm

30"
76 cm

Sleeve

11¼"
28.5 cm

26½"
67.5 cm

RIGHT FRONT

With CC2 and larger needle, CO 3 sts. Purl 1 row. *Next row:* (RS) [K1f&b (see Glossary, page 121)] 2 times, k1—5 sts. Cont as foll:

Row 1: (WS) P1f&b (see Glossary, page 121), purl to last 2 sts, p1f&b, p1—2 sts inc'd.

Row 2: K1f&b, knit to last 2 sts, k1f&b, k1—2 sts inc'd.

Row 3: Purl.

Row 4: K1f&b, knit to last 2 sts, k1f&b, k1—2 sts inc'd.

Row 5: P1f&b, purl to last 2 sts, p1f&b, p1—2 sts inc'd.

Row 6: Knit.

Rep Rows 1–6 (8 sts inc'd every 6 rows) 4 more times, then work Rows 1–5 once more—53 sts; side edge measures about 8" (20.5 cm). With MC, work Rows 6 and 1, then with CC1 work Rows 2–6 and then Row 1, then with MC work Rows 2 and 3—65 sts; side edge measures about 10" (25.5 cm).

Decrease for Side Edge

Row 1: (RS) With CC2, k1, k2tog, knit to last 2 sts, k1f&b, k1—no change in stitch count.

Row 2: P1f&b, purl to last 3 sts, p2tog, p1.

Row 3: Knit.

Row 4: P1f&b, purl to last 3 sts, p2tog, p1.

Row 5: K1, k2tog, knit to last 2 sts, k1f&b, k1.

Row 6: Purl.

Rep Rows 1–6 (increasing on the center front edge and decreasing on the side edge for 2 consecutive rows then working 1 row even) and *at the same time*, when 18 rows of CC2 have been worked, change colors as foll: 2 rows MC, 6 rows CC3, 2 rows MC, 18 rows CC1, 2 rows MC, 6 rows CC2, 2 rows MC, 18 rows CC1, 2 rows MC, 6 rows CC4, 2 rows MC, 18 rows CC3, 2 rows MC, 6 rows CC1, 2 rows MC, 17 rows CC4. *Next row:* Purl with CC4 regardless of where you are in the shaping sequence. Change to MC.

Decrease for Bottom Edge

Row 1: (RS) K1, k2tog, knit to last 3 sts, ssk, k1—2 sts dec'd.

Row 2: P1, ssp (see Glossary, page 120), purl to last 3 sts p2tog, p1—2 sts dec'd.

Row 3: With CC3, knit.

Row 4: P1, ssp, purl to last 3 sts p2tog, p1—2 sts dec'd.

Row 5: K1, k2tog, knit to last 3 sts, ssk, k1—2 sts dec'd.

Row 6: Purl.

Rep Rows 1–6, working 6 rows of CC3, then 2 rows MC, then work with CC1 until 5 sts rem. *Next row:* With CC1, k1, sl 2 sts tog kwise, k1, p2sso, k1—3 sts rem. *Next row:* P3tog. Cut yarn and pull tail through rem st to secure.

LEFT FRONT

CO and work as for right front until there are 65 sts—side edge measures about 10" (25.5 cm).

Decrease for Side Edge

Row 1: (RS) With CC2, k1f&b, knit to last 3 sts, ssk, k1.

Row 2: P1, ssp, purl to last 2 sts, p1f&b, p1.

Row 3: Knit.

Row 4: P1, ssp, purl to last 2 sts, p1f&b, p1.

Row 5: K1f&b, knit to last 3 sts ssk, k1.

Row 6: Purl.

Rep Rows 1–6, working color sequence as for right front, ending with 18 rows of CC4. Decrease for bottom edge and finish as for right front.

BACK

With CC1 and larger needle, CO 3 sts. Purl 1 row. *Next row:* (RS) [K1f&b] 2 times, k1—5 sts. *Next row:* [P1f&b] 4 times, p1—9 sts.

Next row: K4, place marker (pm), k1 (center st), pm, k4. Purl 1 row.

Row 1: (RS) K1f&b, knit to 1 st before m, k1f&b, k1f&b in center st and move second m to between the 2 sts of this inc, knit to last 2 sts, k1f&b, k1—4 sts inc'd.

Row 2: P1f&b, purl to 1 st before m, p1f&b, p1f&b in center st and move second m to between the 2 sts of this inc, purl to last 2 sts, p1f&b, p1—4 sts inc'd.

Row 3: Knit.

Row 4: P1f&b, purl to 1 st before m, p1f&b, p1f&b in center st and move second m as before, purl to last 2 sts, p1f&b, p1—4 sts inc'd.

Row 5: K1f&b, knit to 1 st before m, k1f&b, k1f&b in center st and move second m as before, knit to last 2 sts, k1f&b, k1—4 sts inc'd.

Row 6: Purl.

Rep Rows 1–6 and *at the same time*, change colors as foll: work 2 rows MC, work CC2 until there are 129 sts (64 sts each edge before m), ending with Row 2, then work 2 rows MC, 6 rows CC1, 2 rows MC—153 sts total; 76 sts each edge before m, 1 center st.

Decrease for Side Edge

Change to CC2 and cont to inc at center as before and *at the same time*, dec at side edges as foll:

Row 1: (RS) K1, k2tog, knit to 1 st before m, k1f&b, slip marker (sl m), k1f&b in center st and move second m as before, knit to last 3 sts, ssk, k1.

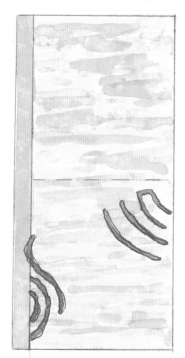

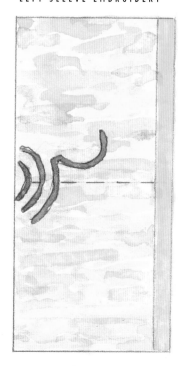

LEFT SLEEVE EMBROIDERY

Row 2: P1, ssp, purl to 1 st before m, p1f&b, sl m, p1f&b and move second m as before, purl to last 3 sts, p2tog, p1.

Row 3: Knit.

Row 4: P1, ssp, purl to 1 st before m, p1f&b, sl m, p1f&b and move second m as before, purl to last 3 sts, p2tog, p1.

Row 5: K1, k2tog, knit to 1 st before m, k1f&b, sl m, k1f&b in center st and move second m as before, knit to last 3 sts, ssk, k1.

Row 6: Purl.

Rep Rows 1–6 and when 18 rows of CC2 are complete, cont shaping while changing colors as foll: 2 rows MC, 6 rows CC3, 2 rows MC, 18 rows CC1, 2 rows MC, 6 rows CC2, 2 rows MC, 18 rows CC1, 2 rows MC, 6 rows CC4, 2 rows MC, 18 rows CC3, 2 rows MC, 6 rows CC1, 2 rows MC, ending with Row 4.

Lower Left Corner

Change to CC4. *Next row:* (RS) K1, k2tog, knit to 1 st before m, k1f&b, remove m, k1f&b, place last inc'd st plus next 76 sts on holder for right corner—77 sts on holder, 77 sts rem for left corner.

Row 1: (WS) P1, ssp, purl to last 3 sts, p2tog, p1—2 sts dec'd.

Row 2: Knit.

Row 3: P1, ssp, purl to last 3 sts, p2tog, p1—2 sts dec'd.

Row 4: K1, k2tog, knit to last 3 sts, ssk, k1—2 sts dec'd.

Row 5: Purl.

Row 6: K1, k2tog, knit to last 3 sts, ssk, k1—2 sts dec'd.

Cont in this manner, dec 1 st each end of needle for 2 consecutive rows, then work 1 row even, until 18 rows of CC4 have been worked, then change colors as foll: 2 rows MC, 6 rows CC3, 2 rows MC, then work with CC1 until 5 sts rem. *Next row:* K1, sl 2 sts tog kwise, k1, p2sso, k1—3 sts rem. P3tog—1 st rem. Cut yarn and pull tail through rem st to secure.

Lower Right Corner

Place 77 sts from holder onto larger needle with RS facing. *Next row:* (RS) With CC4, sl 1, k2tog, knit to last 3 sts, ssk, k1—2 sts dec'd. Beg with Row 1, work as for lower left corner.

SLEEVES

With MC and larger needle, CO 48 sts. Work even in St st until piece measures 30" (76 cm) from CO. BO all sts.

Border

With CC1 and RS facing, pick up and knit 127 sts along one long edge. Knit 1 (WS) row. Work in St st for 8 rows. Knit 3 rows. With WS facing, BO all sts kwise.

NECKBAND

With MC and smaller needle, CO 15 sts.

Row 1: (RS) *K1, p1; rep from * to last st, k1.

Row 2: (WS) *P1, k1; rep from * to last st, p1.

Rep Rows 1 and 2 until piece measures about 88" (223.5 cm)—piece should extend from the lower right front, across the back neck, and down to the lower left front when slightly stretched. BO all sts.

FINISHING

Join Shoulders

With CC2 threaded on a tapestry needle, RS facing, and using the mattress st with a half-st seam allowance (see Glossary, page 123), sew fronts to back at shoulders.

Sleeve embroidery

With crochet hook and CC2, work chain st embroidery (see Glossary, page 120) on front of right sleeve and shoulder of left sleeve following diagrams at left.

Side and Sleeve Seams

With CC1, RS facing, and beg at lower edge, use the mattress st with a half-st seam allowance to sew side seams for about 28" (71 cm), ending at the top edge of a wide CC1 stripe. Sew sleeve seams, matching CO to BO edges. Use the mattress st to seam CC1 sleeve border. Pin midpoint of sleeve to shoulder seam, then down the front and back for 11½" (29 cm). Use the mattress st to sew sleeve into armhole, leaving the bottom 3½" (9 cm) of sleeve free.

Neckband

Pin neckband from lower right front, around the back neck, and down to the lower left front, stretching slightly so that neckband will lay flat. Use the mattress st with a half-st seam allowance to sew in place. Steam seams. Block, using the steam or wet-towel method (see Glossary,

Japanese architecture harmonizes with the environment,

weather, and geography. Traditional Japanese interiors are the embodiment of serenity and embrace the idea of "man with nature"—that is, man living in accord with his natural world. The focus is on simplicity that allows a visual flow through an uncluttered space. Traditionally, the interior color palette reflects the natural outside world.

The yarn I chose for this kimono is a blend of pale natural colors that represent the reflection of sunlight as water trickles over a rocky streambed. The concept of flowing water is enhanced by the curved lower edge and wave stitch pattern. The result is a fluid expression of elegant beauty. The yarn, a blend of rayon and silk, represents the dichotomy between the plant-based fibers used by commoners and the silk used by the upper class. I worked this airy kimono in an open pattern stitch and relatively loose gauge to encourage the supple hand of the flowing fabric. Proportionally, this kimono silhouette is much wider in the body than is traditional. The sleeves are quite short and function like glorified cuffs to stabilize the garment about the arms and shoulders.

MATERIALS

FINISHED SIZE
About 73½" (186.5 cm) in circumference —71¼" (181 cm) garment plus a 2¼" (5.5 cm) space at center front—and 42" (106.5 cm) in length at longest point.

YARN
Worsted weight (#4 Medium).
Shown here: Classic Elite Fame (85% rayon, 15% silk; 115 yd [105 m]/50 g): #1466 Shantung beige (MC), 20 skeins. Classic Elite Provence (100% mercerized Egyptian cotton; 205 yd [187 m]/100 g): #2616 natural (CC), 2 skeins.

NEEDLES
Body and sleeves—size 9 (5.5 mm): 24" (60 cm) circular (cir); neckband—size 6 (4 mm): 40" (100 cm) cir. Adjust needle size if necessary to obtain the correct gauge.

NOTIONS
Stitch holders; markers (m), 2 of which are distinct; knitter's pins; tapestry needle.

GAUGE
17 stitches and 22 rows = 4" (10 cm) in stockinette stitch with MC on larger needle; 17 stitches = 4" (10 cm) in garter stitch with CC on smaller needle.

WATER & SKY

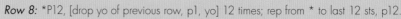

STITCH GUIDE

Right Wave Stitch

(multiple of 24 stitches + 12)

Rows 1 and 2: With MC, knit.
   (*Note:* Drop all yarnovers off needle
   in subsequent repeats of Row 1.)

Rows 3 and 4: With CC, knit.

Rows 5 and 6: With MC, knit.

Row 7: *K12, [k1, yo] 12 times; rep from
   * to last 12 sts, k12.

Row 8: *P12, [drop yo of previous row, p1, yo] 12 times; rep from * to last 12 sts, p12.

Row 9: With MC, knit, dropping each yo of previous row.

Rows 10–14: Repeat Rows 2–6.

Row 15: *[K1, yo] 12 times, k12; rep from * to last 12 sts, [k1, yo] 12 times.

Row 16: *[Drop yo of previous row, p1, yo] 12 times, p12; rep from * to last 24 sts, [drop yo
   of previous row, p1, yo] 12 times.

Repeat Rows 1–16 for pattern.

Left Wave Stitch

(multiple of 24 stitches + 12)

Rows 1 and 2: With MC, knit. (*Note:* Drop all yarnovers off needle in
   subsequent repeats of Row 1.)

Rows 3 and 4: With CC, knit.

Rows 5 and 6: With MC, knit.

Row 7: *[K1, yo] 12 times, k12; rep from * to last 12 sts,
   [k1, yo] 12 times.

Row 8: *[Drop yo of previous row, p1, yo] 12 times, p12; rep from *
   to last 24 sts, [drop yo of previous row, p1, yo] 12 times.

Row 9: With MC, knit, dropping each yo of previous row.

Rows 10–14: Repeat Rows 2–6.

Row 15: *K12, [k1, yo] 12 times; rep from * to last 12 sts, k12.

Row 16: *P12, [drop yo of previous row, p1, yo] 12 times; rep from *
   to last 12 sts, p12.

Repeat Rows 1–16 for pattern.

Center Wave Stitch

(multiple of 24 stitches)

Rows 1 and 2: With MC, knit. (*Note:* Drop all yarnovers off needle in
   subsequent repeats of Row 1.)

Rows 3 and 4: With CC, knit.

Rows 5 and 6: With MC, knit.

Row 7: *[K1, yo] 12 times, k12; rep from *.

Row 8: *P12, [drop yo of previous row, p1, yo] 12 times; rep from *.

Row 9: With MC, knit, dropping each yo of previous row.

Rows 10–14: Repeat Rows 2–6.

Row 15: *K12, [k1, yo] 12 times; rep from *.

Row 16: *[Drop yo of previous row, p1, yo] 12 times, p12;
   rep from *.

Repeat Rows 1–16 for pattern.

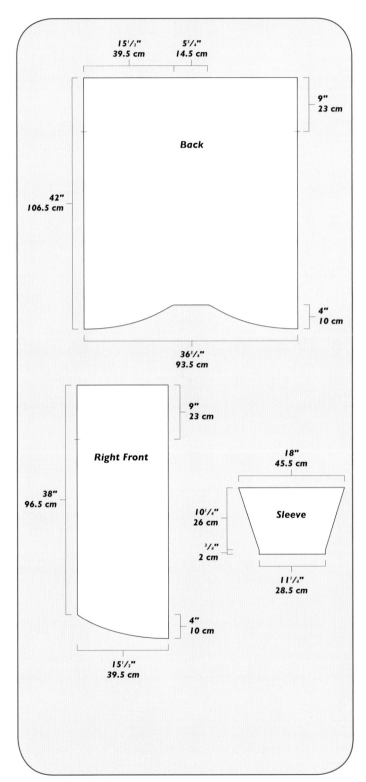

RIGHT FRONT

With MC and larger needle, CO 66 sts.

Row 1: (RS) K5 (edge sts), place marker (pm), k60, pm, k1 (edge st).

Row 2: Knit, slipping markers (sl m) when you come to them.

Work Rows 3–6 of right wave st patt (see Stitch Guide), working center 60 sts in right wave st patt and edge sts in garter st (knit every row).

Shaping row: (RS; Row 7 of patt) Knit (if necessary) to 2 sts before first m, k2tog, work in right wave st patt to next m, k1f&b (see Glossary, page 121), knit (if necessary) to end. Cont in patt, rep shaping row every 8th row 3 more times—1 st before first m, 5 sts after last m. Work even for 7 more rows, ending with Row 6 of patt—38 rows total (2 full reps of patt plus 6 rows); piece measures about 6½" (16.5 cm) from CO at longest point.

Shape Lower Curve

Cont in St st, work short-rows (see Glossary, page 124) as foll:

Short-Rows 1 and 2: K6, wrap next st, turn work, p6. Do not hide wraps on foll rows.

Short-Rows 3 and 4: K12, wrap next st, turn, p12.

Short-Rows 5 and 6: K18, wrap next st, turn, p18.

Cont to work short-rows in this manner, working 6 more sts in each short-row pair until all 66 sts have been worked.

Upper Body

Cont even in St st on all sts until piece measures 42" (106.5 cm) from lower center front edge. Place all sts on holder.

LEFT FRONT

With MC, CO 66 sts.

Row 1: K1 (edge st), pm, k60, pm, k5 (edge sts). Sl m every row.

Row 2: Knit all sts.

Work Rows 3–6 of right wave st patt (see Stitch Guide), working center 60 sts in right wave st patt and edge sts in garter st. *Shaping row:* (RS; Row 7 of patt) Knit (if necessary) to 1 st before first m, k1f&b, work in right wave st patt to next m, k2tog, knit (if necessary) to end. Cont in patt, rep shaping row every 8th row 3 more times—5 sts before first m, 1 st after last m. Work even for 7 more rows, ending with Row 6 of patt—38 rows total (2 full reps of patt plus 6 rows); piece measures about 6½" (16.5 cm) from CO at longest point.

Shape Lower Curve

Cont in St st, knit 1 (RS) row. Work short-rows to mirror right front as foll:

Short-Rows 1 and 2: P6, wrap next st, turn work, k6. Do not hide wraps on foll rows.

THE CONCEPT OF FLOWING WATER

is enhanced by the curved lower

edge and wave stitch pattern.

The result is a fluid expression

of elegant beauty.

Short-Rows 3 and 4: P12, wrap next st, turn, k12.

Short-Rows 5 and 6: P18, wrap next st, turn, k18.

Cont to work short-rows in this manner, working 6 more sts in each short-row pair until all 66 sts have been worked.

Upper Body

Cont even in St st until piece measures 42" (106.5 cm) from lower center front edge. Place all sts on holder.

BACK

With MC, CO 156 sts. The first 66 sts will be worked the same as for the right front, the center 24 sts will be worked in center wave st patt (see Stitch Guide), and the last 66 sts will be worked using the left wave stitch patt as foll:

Row 1: K5, pm, work 60 sts in right wave st patt, pm, k1, place distinct m, work 24 sts in center wave st patt, place second distinct m, k1, pm, work 60 sts in left wave st patt, pm, k5. Sl m every row.

Work Rows 2–6 of wave st patts, working all non-wave st patt sts in garter st as established. *Shaping row:* (RS; Row 7 of patts) Knit (if necessary) to 2 sts before first m, k2tog, work in right wave st patt to next m, k1f&b, knit (if necessary) to first distinct m, work in center wave st patt to next distinct m, knit (if necessary) to 1 st before next m, k1f&b, work in left wave st patt to next m, k2tog, knit (if necessary) to end. Cont in patt, rep shaping row every 8th row 3 more times—1 st before first m, 1 st after last m, 5 sts before first distinct m, 5 sts after second distinct m. Work even for 7 more rows, ending with Row 6 of patts—38 rows total (2 full reps of patt plus 6 rows); piece measures about 6½" (16.5 cm) from CO at longest point.

Shape Lower Curve

Cont in St st, work short-rows on right back as foll:

Short-Rows 1 and 2: K6, wrap next st, turn work, p6. Do not hide wraps on foll rows.

Short-Rows 3 and 4: K12, wrap next st, turn, p12.

Short-Rows 5 and 6: K18, wrap next st, turn, p18.

Cont to work short-rows in this manner, working 6 more sts in each short-row pair until all 66 sts before first distinct m have been worked. Knit 1 RS row.

Work short-rows on left back as foll:

Short-Rows 1 and 2: P6, wrap next st, turn work, k6. Do not hide wraps on foll rows.

Short-Rows 3 and 4: P12, wrap next st, turn, k12.

Short-rows 5 and 6: P18, wrap next st, turn, k18.

Cont to work short-rows in this manner, working 6 more sts in each short-row pair until all 66 sts before distinct m have been worked. Purl 1 WS row.

Cont even in St st until piece measures 42" (106.5 cm) from lower edge of curved sections. Leave sts on needle.

JOIN SHOULDERS

Place 66 right front sts onto a needle. With RS tog, use the three-needle method (see Glossary, page 117) to BO 66 right front sts tog with 66 back sts for right shoulder, BO the next 24 back sts for back neck, place 66 left front sts onto a needle and BO 66 left front sts tog with rem 66 back sts for left shoulder.

SLEEVES

Measure down 9" (23 cm) from shoulder seam on front and back at side edges and place markers. With MC, larger needle, and RS facing, pick up and knit 76 sts between markers. Knit 1 (WS) row. Work in St st, dec 1 st each end of needle every 4th row 14 times, ending with a WS row—48 sts rem. Change to CC and smaller needle and knit 2 rows. Change to MC and knit 2 rows. Change to CC and knit 1 row. BO all sts kwise.

NECKBAND

With CC and smaller needle, CO 379 sts. Knit 3 rows. Change to MC and knit 2 rows. Change to CC and knit 2 rows. Change to MC and knit 4 rows. Change to CC and knit 2 rows. Change to MC and knit 2 rows. Change to CC and knit 3 rows. Loosely BO all sts kwise.

FINISHING

Side and Sleeve Seams

Pin sides and sleeves tog with WS tog so that the bottom of the side front aligns with the top of the wave stitch pattern on back. (The hemline waves down in center front and up at side front; down at side back and up at center back.) With MC threaded on a tapestry needle, use the mattress stitch (see Glossary, page 123) to sew side and sleeve seams.

Neckband

Pin neckband around center fronts and back neck. With MC threaded on a tapestry needle, use a whipstitch (see Glossary, page 124) to sew in place.

Using the wet-towel method (see Glossary, page 117), block to measurements. Allow to thoroughly air-dry.

Taiko Happi

Happi coats originated as Japanese loose overcoats of

unlined cotton with the family crest or emblem on the upper back. They were everyday short coats worn by workers with somewhat fitted pants for men or with very loose pants and aprons for women. Today happi coats are widely used for festivals, or *matsuri*, and many feature bold graphic images. Simple and plain sleeveless happi are worn by *Taiko* drummers performing at festivals.

Shibori is the Japanese word for a variety of resist dyeing techniques in which cloth is folded, stitched, bound, or sheathed in numerous combinations to protect areas from dye penetration when submerged in a vat of dye. Chance and accident give life to the shibori process, and are its special magic and strongest appeal.

I have combined happi and shibori inspirations into this classic styled vest. I worked linen yarn in a crossed herringbone stitch that produces a stable fabric that has beautiful drape when pressed with a hot iron. The neckband is worked in a slip-stitch pattern that has the understated elegance of traditional shibori.

MATERIALS

FINISHED SIZE
About 45½" (115.5 cm) in circumference—44" (112 cm) garment plus a 1½" (3.8 cm) space at center front—and 21" (53.5 cm) in length.

YARN
Sportweight (#2 Fine).
Shown here: Louet Euroflax Originals (100% wet-spun linen; 270 yd [247 m]/100 g): #18.44 sandalwood (MC), 4 skeins; #18.22 black (CC), 1 skein.

NEEDLES
Body—size 6 (4 mm): 32" (80 cm) circular (cir). Borders—size 4 (3.5 mm): 24" and 32" (60 cm and 80 cm) and size 3 (3.25 mm): 32" (80 cm) cir. Adjust needle size if necessary to obtain the correct gauge.

NOTIONS
4 open-ring markers (m); large stitch holders; knitters' pins; tapestry needle.

GAUGE
30 stitches and 28 rows = 4" (10 cm) in horizontal herringbone pattern on largest needle.

TAIKO HAPPI

Horizontal Herringbone
(even number of sts)

Row 1: (RS) K1, *sl 1 pwise, k1, psso
but do not drop off left needle, knit
into back of slipped st, drop st off
needle; rep from * to last st, k1.

Row 2: *P2tog but do not drop off
needle, purl into front of first st, drop
both sts off needle; rep from * to
end of row.

Repeat Rows 1 and 2 for pattern.

Bind Off in Pattern

K1, *sl 1 pwise, k1, psso but do not drop off left needle, BO second st on right needle by
passing it over first st and dropping it off the needle, knit into back of passed sl st and remove
it from needle, BO by passing second st on right needle over first and dropping off needle;
rep from * to 1 st before m or to last 2 sts on left needle, k1, BO by passing second st over
first and dropping off, k1 (first st after m or last st on left needle), BO by passing second st over
first and dropping off the needle.

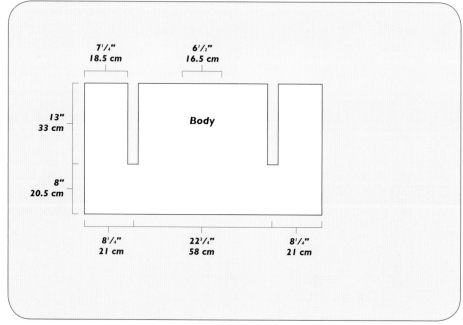

7¼"
18.5 cm

6½"
16.5 cm

13"
33 cm

Body

8"
20.5 cm

8¼"
21 cm

22¾"
58 cm

8¼"
21 cm

BODY

With MC, largest needle, and using the long-tail method (see Glossary, page 118), CO 292 sts. Work Row 2 of horizontal herringbone patt (see Stitch Guide) across all sts. Rep Rows 1 and 2 of patt until piece measures 8" (20.5 cm) from CO, ending with a WS row.

Divide for Armholes

Place open-ring markers (pm) on needle (without working any sts) as foll: 54 sts for right front, pm, 14 sts for right armhole, pm, 156 sts for back, pm, 14 sts for left armhole, pm, 54 sts for left front—4 markers placed. *Next row:* (RS) K1, rep from * to * of Row 1 of patt across 52 right front sts, k1—54 sts on right-hand needle for right front; BO 14 sts in patt for armhole (see Stitch Guide)—1 st rem on right-hand needle for back; rep from * to * of Row 1 of patt across next 154 sts, k1—156 sts for back; BO 14 sts in patt for armhole—1 st rem on right-hand needle for left front; rep from * to * of Row 1 of patt across next 52 sts, k1—54 sts for left front. Place 156 back sts on one holder and 54 right front sts on a second holder.

Left Front

Cont in patt on 54 left front sts until armhole measures 13" (33 cm), ending with a WS row. BO all sts in patt.

Back

Place 156 back sts onto largest needle. With WS facing, join MC at right edge of work and, beg with Row 2, cont in patt until armholes measure 13" (33 cm), ending with a WS row. BO all sts in patt.

Right Front

Place 54 held right front sts onto largest needle. With WS facing, join MC at right edge of work and, beg with Row 2, cont in patt until armhole measures 13" (33 cm), ending with a WS row. BO all sts in patt.

FINISHING

Join Shoulders

Fold garment with RS tog, matching armhole edges at shoulders. Pin shoulders tog. With MC threaded on a tapestry needle, use a whipstitch (see Glossary, page 124) to sew shoulder seams. Press with hot iron (set for linen) on both sides of work to flatten.

Armhole Border

With CC, 24" (60 cm) middle-size cir needle, RS facing, and beg at lower back armhole, pick up and knit 69 sts along back, 69 sts along front, and 12 sts across underarm—150 sts total. Join for working in the rnd. Firmly BO all sts pwise. Repeat for left armhole.

Front Border

With CC, smallest cir needle, RS facing, and beg at right center front lower corner, pick up and knit 136 sts along right front edge, 47 sts across back neck, and 136 sts along left front edge—319 sts total. Knit 1 row. Cut CC, leaving a 36" (91.5 cm) tail to work selvedge st in garter st. With RS facing and using the intarsia method of crossing yarns at color changes to avoid holes, k1 with CC tail, change to MC, knit to last st, rejoin CC, k1. With WS facing, change to middle-size needle and beg check patt as foll, crossing yarns at color changes:

Row 1: (WS) With CC, k1, p1, *sl 1 with yarn in front (wyf), p1; rep from * to last st, k1.

Row 2: (RS) With CC, k1, p1, *sl 1 with yarn in back (wyb), p1; rep from * to last st, k1.

Rows 3 and 4: With CC, k1, change to MC, purl to last st, with CC, k1. Work Rows 1–4 a total of 6 times, then work Rows 1–2 once more. Change to smallest needle and work Rows 3–4 again. Change to CC and purl 1 row. With RS facing, firmly BO all sts pwise.

Blocking

With hot iron set for linen, press body of garment, including armhole borders; do not press neckband. Steam neckband and stretch to eliminate puckers along front edge. Lay flat to thoroughly air-dry.

Kabuki Theater Squares

Kabuki theater originated from *kabuki odori*, a kind of dance

performed in Kyoto in the early Edo period (seventeenth century) by the dancer Okuni of the Izumo region. All male and female roles are performed by men and the drama is enhanced by song and dance. Kabuki became a hub of social activity during a time when merchants and a lively urban populace gained affluence and more disposable income. Artists were commissioned to create ever more lavish and flamboyant kosode. The rich opulence of the stage found its way into everyday wardrobes, with a visual vocabulary of bold patterns of stripes and checks.

This kimono features intarsia checks in a palette of warm wood tones in a matte linen yarn that yields exquisite drape when pressed. The checkered pattern is framed by the neckband and hem borders of a bold slip-stitch chevron pattern. This knitting adventure is time intensive, but the end result is worth the effort.

MATERIALS

FINISHED SIZE
About 57½" (146 cm) in circumference—56¼" (143 cm) garment plus a 1¼" (3.2 cm) space at center front—and 40" (101.5 cm) in length.

YARN
Sportweight (#2 Fine).
Shown here: Louet Euroflax Originals (100% wet-spun linen; 270 yd [247 m]/100 g): tobacco, 5 skeins; black, 3 skeins; cedarwood, mustard, and champagne, 2 skeins each.

NEEDLES
Size 4 (3.5 mm): two 32" (80 cm) circular (cir). Adjust needle size if necessary to obtain the correct gauge.

NOTIONS
23 markers (m); knitter's pins; tapestry needle.

GAUGE
22 stitches and 28 rows = 4" (10 cm) in stockinette stitch.

KABUKI THEATER SQUARES

NOTES

- The body is knitted in one piece from hem to shoulder. The sleeves are knitted separately. The neckband and sleeve bands are picked up and knitted from the body and sleeves.

The colored squares are worked in the intarsia method with a separate length of yarn for each square. Each square will take about 3½ yards (3.2 meters) of yarn.

Each square on the Squares and Sleeve charts represents 12 stitches and 14 rows. Weave in the yarn ends periodically as you go so there won't be so many when the garment is finished.

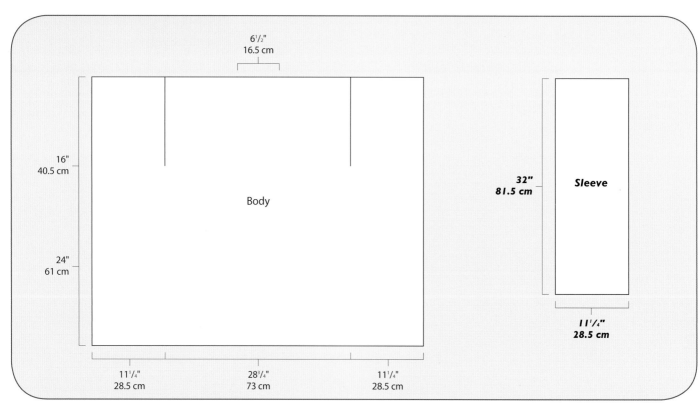

SQUARES

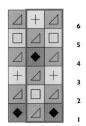

SLEEVE

lower back

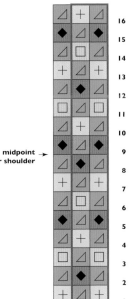

midpoint
for shoulder →

lower front

■ with black, k on RS, p on WS

◿ with tobacco, k on RS, p on WS

◆ with cedarwood, k on RS, p on WS

+ with mustard, k on RS, p on WS

□ with champagne, k on RS, p on WS

∨ sl with yarn at WS

☐ pattern repeat

ZEBRA CHEVRON

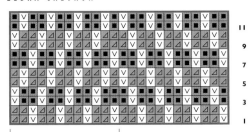

end
sleeve

end
body

BACK AND FRONT

With black, CO 278 sts. Knit 1 (WS) row. Keeping the first and last st in garter st, work center 276 sts according to Zebra Chevron chart, ending as indicated for body, working Rows 1–12 two times. Cut off tobacco. Knit 1 (RS) row with black, then cut off black. Do not turn; slide all sts to opposite end of needle in preparation for squares patt. Work Rows 1–6 of Squares chart (see Notes) once, then work Rows 1–5 once more—11 rows of squares total; piece measures about 24" (61 cm) from CO.

Divide for Underarm

Cont as charted, work across the first 5 squares (61 sts, including selvedge st) for the right front, and *at the same time* work k1f&b (see Glossary, page 121) in the 12th st of the fifth square—62 sts for right front. Join appropriate color for next square but do not wrap it around the previous yarn so that the back will be separate from the right front, k1f&b in the first st, then work as charted across 13 squares (155 more sts), and *at the same time* work k1f&b in the last st of the thirteenth square—158 sts for back. Join appropriate color for next square but do not wrap it around the previous yarn so that the left front will be separate from the back, k1f&b in the first st, then work as charted across rem 60 sts—62 sts for left front.

Cont as charted, knitting the first and last st of each piece, until 8 more rows of squares have been worked—19 rows of squares total; piece measures 40" (101.5 cm) from CO.

Join Shoulders

Place 62 right front sts on separate needle. Fold kimono at right side seam matching front and back shoulders with RS tog. Use the three-needle method (see Glossary, page 117) to BO 60 sts of right front tog with 60 sts of back, then work the last 2 sts of front tog with 1 st from back to complete final square. BO the next 36 back sts for the back neck. Place 62 left front sts on separate needle. Fold kimono at left side seam matching front and back shoulders together with RS tog, and use the three-needle method to BO rem sts tog, working the first 2 sts of the front tog with 1 st from back to align the first square.

SLEEVES

With tobacco, CO 62 sts. Keeping first and last st in garter st, work center 60 sts according to Sleeve chart, binding off on last (WS) row of squares.

Border

With black, RS facing, and beg at BO end for right sleeve and at CO end for left sleeve, pick up and knit 1 st in BO or CO edge, 12 sts in each square along 16-square length, and 1 st in CO or BO edge—194 sts total. Knit 1 (WS) row. Keeping first and last st in garter st, work center 192 sts according to Zebra Chevron chart, ending as indicated for sleeve, working Rows 1–12 two times. Cut off tobacco. With black, knit 1 (RS) row. With WS facing, BO all sts kwise. With tobacco and using the invisible horizontal method (see Glossary, page 122), graft sleeve seam, joining CO to BO edge of each square. Use the mattress st with 1-st seam allowance (see Glossary, page 123) to seam the border.

FINISHING

Front Band

With black, RS facing, and beg at right center front lower edge, pick up and knit 13 sts in lower border, 12 sts in each square along right front to shoulder seam, 12 sts in each square across back neck, 12 sts in each square along left front, and 13 sts in lower border—518 sts total. *Next row:* (WS) With second circular needle, knit, placing markers (pm) as foll: k1 (selvedge st; knit every row), pm, [k24, pm] 10 times (10th m is at shoulder seam), k18, pm (center back; use a different colored marker here), k18, pm (shoulder), [k24, pm] 10 times, k1 (selvedge st; knit every row). Work with both circular needles to accommodate all sts more easily. Work zebra chevron patt as foll, slipping markers (sl m) as you come to them:

Row 1: (RS) With tobacco, k1, *sl 1, k2; rep from * to last st, k1.

Row 2: With tobacco, k1, *p2, sl 1; rep from * to last st, k1.

Row 3: With black, k1, *k1, sl 1, [k2, sl 1] 3 times, k3, [sl 1 k2] 3 times, sl 1*, rep from * to * 9 more times, k1, sl 1, [k2, sl 1] 3 times, k3, sl 1, k2, sl 1 (center back), k1, sl 1, k2, sl 1, k3, [sl 1, k2] 3 times, sl 1, work from * to * 10 times, k1.

Row 4: With black, k1, purl the black sts and slip the tobacco sts to the last st, k1.

Row 5: With tobacco, k1, *k2, [sl 1, k2] 3 times, sl 1, k1, sl 1, [k2, sl 1] 3 times, k1*, rep from * to * 9 more times, k2, [sl 1, k2] 3 times, sl 1, k1, sl 1, k2, sl 1, k1, (center back), k2, sl 1, k2, sl 1, k1, sl 1, [k2, sl 1] 3 times, k1, work from * to * 10 times, k1.

The rich opulence of the stage found its way

into everyday wardrobes,

with a visual vocabulary of bold patterns

of stripes and checks.

Row 6: With tobacco, k1, purl the tobacco sts and slip the black sts to the last st, k1.

Rows 7 and 8: With black, rep Rows 1 and 2.

Rows 9 and 10: With tobacco, rep Rows 3 and 4.

Rows 11 and 12: With black, rep Rows 5 and 6.

Rep Rows 1–12 once more. Cut off tobacco. Knit 1 row with black. With WS facing, snugly BO all sts kwise.

Join Sleeves

With hot iron, lightly press sleeves and body selvedge edges to make it easier to sew together. Match midpoint of sleeve to shoulder seam and pin tog for 5 squares down from shoulder on both front and back. With tobacco, use the mattress st to sew sleeves to armholes. At side of body, sew tog 12th and 13th rows of squares on front and back to make a firm side seam.

Blocking

With a hot iron set for linen, press hard over entire garment on both RS and WS to flatten the knitting and give it drape, taking care not to pull or stretch needlessly (the kimono will measure slightly larger after pressing).

Samurai Jinbaori

The *jinbaori* started as surcoats worn over armor by military

commanders during the Warring States period from the late fourteenth to the nineteenth century. They later became short battle jackets. Daring and unconventional designs were often used for jinbaori, incorporating materials such as rash and *kinran* (silk patterned by gilt paper strip). Knotted cords called the "dragonfly knot" were sometimes added to the back, suggesting a warrior's bravery in not retreating.

Curved armholes, stand-up collars, and tie closures were common jinbaori features. In my version, I've exaggerated the armhole curve outward at the shoulder. I've also added curves to the front and back lower edges. The black silk with a white collar and red trim is a color triad that commands attention in a dramatic visual statement.

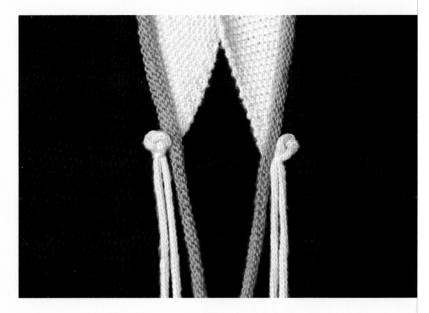

MATERIALS

FINISHED SIZE
About 44" (112 cm) in circumference —40½" (103 cm) garment plus a 3½" (9 cm) space at center front—22" (56 cm) in length.

YARN
DK weight (#3 Light).
Shown here: Debbie Bliss Pure Silk (100% silk; 137 yd [125 m]/ 50 g): #27001 black (MC), 8 skeins; #27003 cream, 2 skeins; #27012 lipstick, 1 skein.

NEEDLES
Body and sleeves—size 5 (3.75 mm): 24" (60 cm) circular (cir); collar band— size 4 (3.5 mm): straight or cir and set of 4 double-pointed (dpn); optional: size 6 (4 mm) needle to work a loose bind-off. Adjust needle size if necessary to obtain the correct gauge.

NOTIONS
Safety pin; 13 open-ring markers (m); size D/3 (3.25 mm) crochet hook; tapestry needle.

GAUGE
22 stitches and 36 rows = 4" (10 cm) in seed stitch on larger needle.

STITCH GUIDE

Seed Stitch   (odd number of sts)
Row 1: *K1, p1; rep from * to last st, k1.
Repeat Row 1 for pattern.

Seed Stitch   (even number of sts)
Row 1: *K1, p1; rep from *.
Row 2: *P1, k1; rep from *.
Repeat Rows 1 and 2 for pattern.

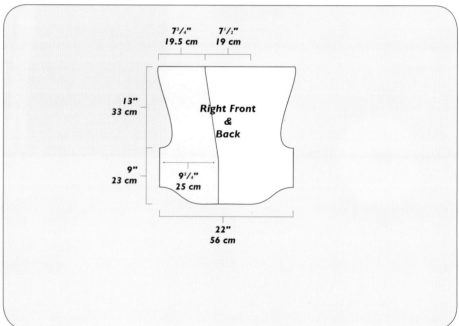

7³/₄"
19.5 cm

7¹/₂"
19 cm

13"
33 cm

**Right Front
&
Back**

9"
23 cm

9³/₄"
25 cm

22"
56 cm

BACK

With MC and larger needle, CO 41 sts. Work 1 (WS) row in seed stitch. Use the cable method (see Glossary, page 118) to CO 9 sts at beg of next (RS) row, then work across all sts in seed st as established—50 sts. Use the cable method to CO 9 sts at beg of next (WS) row, then work across all sts in patt—59 sts. (Note: Because seed st looks the same on both sides, fasten a safety pin to the RS of the work.) At beg of the next 2 rows, use the cable method to CO 7 sts—73 sts. Cont in seed st as established, use the cable method to CO the foll number of sts at beg of every 2 rows as before: 5 sts, 3 sts, 2 sts, [1 st] 4 times (8 rows total), 2 sts, 3 sts, then 5 sts—121 sts when all CO have been worked; piece measures about 2¾" (7 cm) from initial CO. Cont even in seed st until piece measures 9" (23 cm) from initial CO.

Shape Armholes

BO 3 sts at beg of next 2 rows, then BO 2 sts at beg of foll 4 rows—107 sts rem. Dec 1 st each end of needle every other row 4 times—99 sts rem. Cont even until armholes measure 7" (18 cm), ending with a WS row. Inc 1 st each end of needle every other row 7 times, then every 4th row 6 times—125 sts. Cont even in patt until armholes measure 13" (33 cm). BO all sts.

RIGHT FRONT

With MC and larger needle, CO 13 sts. Work 1 (RS) row in seed stitch. Use the cable method to CO 9 sts at beg of next (WS) row, then work across all sts in seed st as established—22 sts. Work 1 (RS) row even. Use the cable method to CO 7 at beg of next (WS) row, then work across all sts in patt—29 sts. Work 1 row even. Cont in seed st as established, use the cable method to CO the foll number of sts at the beg of every WS row as before: 5 sts, 3 sts, 2 sts, [1 st] 4 times, 2 sts, 3 sts, then 5 sts—53 sts when all CO have been worked; piece measures about 2¾" (7 cm) from initial CO. Cont even in seed st until piece measures 7" (18 cm) from initial CO, ending with a WS row.

Shape Neckline and Armhole

Note: The neckline and armhole are shaped at the same time; read through the entire section before beginning. Keeping in patt, dec 1 st at beg of next (RS) row. Work 9 rows even in patt. Rep the last 10 rows 12 more times—13 neckline decs. (Note: It is helpful to mark each dec with an open-ring marker.) At the same time, when piece measures 9" (23 cm) from initial CO, shape armhole as foll: At armhole edge (beg of WS rows), BO 3 sts once, then BO 2 sts 2 times, then dec 1 st every other row 4 times—11 armhole decs. Cont even at armhole edge until armhole measures 7"

(18 cm), then inc 1 st at armhole edge every other row 7 times, then every 4th row 6 times—42 sts rem when all neck and armhole decs and incs have been made. Cont even in seed st until armhole measures 13" (33 cm). BO all sts.

LEFT FRONT

With MC and larger needle, CO 13 sts. Work 1 (WS) row in seed st. Cont in seed st, use the cable method to CO the foll number of sts at beg of RS rows as before: 9 sts, 7 sts, 5 sts, 3 sts, 2 sts, [1 st] 4 times, 2 sts, 3 sts, then 5 sts—53 sts when all CO have been worked; piece measures about 2¾" (7 cm) from initial CO. Cont even in seed st until piece measures 7" (18 cm) from initial CO, ending with a WS row.

Shape Neckline and Armhole

Note: The neckline and armhole are shaped at the same time; read through the entire section before beginning. Keeping in patt, dec 1 st at end of next (RS) row. Work 9 rows even in patt. Rep the last 10 rows 12 more times—13 neckline decs. At the same time, when piece measures 9" (23 cm) from initial CO, shape armhole as foll: At armhole edge (beg of RS rows) BO 3 sts once, then BO 2 sts 2 times, then dec 1 st every other row 4 times—11 armhole decs. Cont even at armhole edge until armhole measures 7" (18 cm). Then inc 1 st at armhole edge every other row 7 times, then every 4th row 6 times—42 sts rem when all neck and armhole decs and incs have been made. Cont even in seed st until armhole measures 13" (33 cm). BO all sts.

COLLAR BAND

With cream and smaller needles, CO 3 sts for lower right collar point.

Set-up row: K1, p1, k1.

Row 1: (RS) K1f&b (see Glossary, page 121), p1, k1—4 sts.

Row 2 and all WS rows: *K1, p1; rep from *, ending k1 if there are an odd number of sts.

Row 3: P1f&b (see Glossary, page 121), k1, p1, k1—5 sts.

Row 5: K1f&b, [p1, k1] 2 times—6 sts.

Row 7: P1f&b, [k1, p1] 2 times, k1—7 sts.

Row 9: K1f&b, *p1, k1; rep from *—8 sts.

Row 11: P1f&b, *k1, p1; rep from * to last st, k1—9 sts.

Rep Rows 9–12 until there are 15 sts, then rep Row 2 until piece measures about 34" (86.5 cm) from CO, ending with a WS row. Dec as foll:

Row 1: (RS) P2tog, work in seed st to end—14 sts rem.

Row 2: *K1, p1; rep from *.

Row 3: K2tog, work in seed st to end—13 sts rem.

Row 4: *K1, p1; rep from * to last st, k1.

Repeat Rows 1–4 until 3 sts rem for lower left collar point. BO all sts.

FINISHING

Shoulder Seams

Pin fronts to back with RS tog and outer shoulder edges aligned. With a crochet hook and using slip-stitch crochet (see Glossary, page 124), join shoulder seams.

Side Seams

With MC threaded on a tapestry needle and using the mattress stitch (see Glossary, page 123), sew side seams.

Crochet Edging

With MC, crochet hook, RS facing, and beg at right center front lower edge, work single crochet (sc; see Glossary, page 119) as foll: 110 sc along right center front, 35 sc across back neck, and 110 sc along left center front. Work 3 sc into corner st to turn, work 55 sc along curved left front lower edge, 136 sc along back curved lower edge, and 55 sc along right front curved lower edge. Join with sl st to first sc. Cut yarn. With MC, crochet hook, RS facing, and beg at underarm, work 75 sc along curved armhole to shoulder and 75 sc along curved armhole to underarm. Check often to make sure you are keeping the work flat. Join with sl st to first sc. Fasten off.

Front Border

With lipstick, larger needle, RS facing, and beg with center sc of lower right front corner, pick up and knit 1 st through back loop of each sc along right front, back neck, and left front, ending with center sc of left front corner—259 sts. Knit 1 row, purl 1 row, knit 1 row. Loosely BO all sts pwise. (*Note:* Use a size 6 needle for the BO if necessary to ensure the BO is not too tight.)

Lower Border

With cream, larger needle, RS facing, and beg with center sc of corner at lower left front, pick up and knit 1 st through back loop of each sc along lower edge, ending with center sc of corner at lower right front—250 sts. Knit 1 row. Loosely BO all sts pwise as before.

Armhole Border

With cream, larger needle, RS facing, and beg at underarm, pick up and knit 1 st in back loop of each sc—150 sts. Place marker (pm) and join for working in the rnd. Purl 1 rnd. Loosely BO all sts pwise.

Apply Collar Band

Mark 15½" (39.5 cm) down from shoulder on each side of front along center front edge; mark center back neck. On collar, mark center of long edge and mark 3" (7.5 cm) from each side of center mark on long edge of collar. Align center of collar to center back neck, align 3" (7.5 cm) marks to shoulder seams, and align collar points to front marks. Pin collar to front behind red edging. With cream, use a whipstitch (see Glossary, page 124) to sew collar to front edge along black sc.

Knitted Cords (make 2)

With cream and dpn, work a 3-st knit-cord (see Glossary, page 121) 20" (51 cm) long. On last row of cord, do not slide sts to other end of needle. Instead, pass second and third st over first and off end of needle. Cut yarn. Pull tail through last loop to secure. Tie a loose first half of a square knot in the middle of the length of cord (Figure 1). Fold in half at the knot (Figure 2) and pin in place on front at lower point of collar. With cream, tack knot into place from WS.

Steam-press to block to measurements.

CORD KNOT

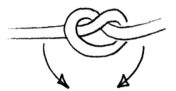

Figure 1

Figure 2

GLOSSARY

beg	beginning; begin; begins		**RS**	right side
BO	bind off		**sl**	slip
CC	contrast color		**sl st**	slip st (slip 1 st pwise unless otherwise indicated)
cm	centimeter(s)		**ssk**	slip, slip, knit
cn	cable needle		**St st**	stockinette stitch
CO	cast on		**tbl**	through back loop
cont	continue(s); continuing		**tog**	together
dec(s)	decrease(s); decreasing		**WS**	wrong side
dpn	double-pointed needles		**wyb**	with yarn in back
foll	follow(s); following		**wyf**	with yarn in front
g	gram(s)		**yd**	yard(s)
inc(s)	increase(s); increasing		**yo**	yarnover
k	knit		*	repeat starting point
k1f&b	knit into the front and back of same st		* *	repeat all instructions between asterisks
kwise	knitwise, as if to knit		( )	alternate measurements and/or instructions
m	marker(s)		[ ]	work instructions as a group a specified number of times
MC	main color			
mm	millimeter(s)			
M1	make one (increase)			
p	purl			
p1f&b	purl into front and back of same st			
patt(s)	pattern(s)			
psso	pass slipped st over			
pwise	purlwise, as if to purl			
rem	remain(s); remaining			
rep	repeat(s); repeating			
rev St st	reverse stockinette stitch			
rnd(s)	round(s)			

BIND-OFFS

Standard Bind-Off

Knit the first stitch, *knit the next stitch (two stitches on right needle), insert left needle tip into first stitch on right needle (Figure 1) and lift this stitch up and over the second stitch (Figure 2) and off the needle (Figure 3). Repeat from * for the desired number of stitches.

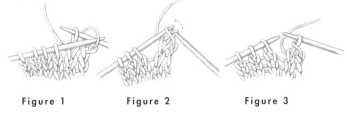

Figure 1   Figure 2   Figure 3

Three-Needle Bind-Off

Place the stitches to be joined onto two separate needles and hold the needles parallel so that the right sides of knitting face together. Insert a third needle into the first stitch on each of two needles (Figure 1) and knit them together as one stitch (Figure 2), *knit the next stitch on each needle the same way, then use the left needle tip to lift the first stitch over the second and off the needle (Figure 3). Repeat from * until no stitches remain on first two needles. Cut yarn and pull tail through last stitch to secure.

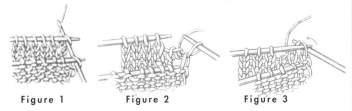

Figure 1   Figure 2   Figure 3

BLOCKING

Steam Blocking

Pin the pieces to be blocked to a blocking surface. Hold an iron set on the steam setting ½" (1.5 cm) above the knitted surface and direct the steam over the entire surface (except ribbing). You can get similar results by lapping wet cheesecloth on top of the knitted surface and touching it lightly with a dry iron. Lift and set down the iron gently; do not use a pushing motion.

Wet-Towel Blocking

Run a large bath or beach towel (or two towels for larger projects) through the rinse/spin cycle of a washing machine. Roll the knitted pieces in the wet towel(s), place the roll in a plastic bag, and leave overnight so that the knitted pieces become uniformly damp. Pin the damp pieces to a blocking surface and let air-dry thoroughly.

BUTTONHOLE

One-Row Buttonhole

Bring the yarn to the front of the work, slip the next stitch purlwise, then return the yarn to the back. *Slip the next stitch, pass the second stitch over the slipped stitch (Figure 1) and drop it off the needle. Repeat from * 2 more times. Slip the last stitch on the right needle to the left needle (Figure 2) and turn the work around. Bring the working yarn to the back, [insert the right needle between the first and second stitches on the left needle, draw up a loop (Figure 3), and place in on the left needle] 4 times. Turn the work around. With the yarn in back, slip the first stitch and pass the extra cast-on stitch over it (Figure 4) and off the needle to complete the buttonhole.

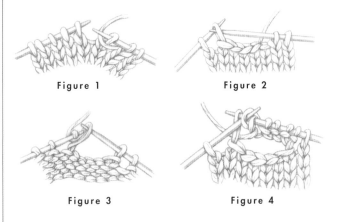

Figure 1   Figure 2

Figure 3   Figure 4

CAST-ONS

Backward-Loop Cast-On

*Loop working yarn and place it on needle backward so that it doesn't unwind. Repeat from *.

Cable Cast-On

Hold needle with stitches in your left hand, *insert right needle *between* the first two stitches on left needle (Figure 1), wrap yarn around needle as if to knit, draw yarn through (Figure 2), and place new loop on left needle (Figure 3) to form a new stitch. Repeat from * for the desired number of stitches, always working between the first two stitches on the left needle.

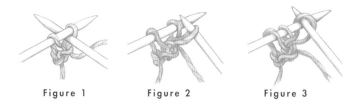

Figure 1   Figure 2   Figure 3

Crochet Chain Provisional Cast-On

With waste yarn and crochet hook, make a loose crochet chain (see page 119) about four stitches more than you need to cast on. With knitting needle, working yarn, and beginning two stitches from end of chain, pick up and knit one stitch through the loop on the back side of each crochet chain for desired number of stitches. When you're ready to work in the opposite direction, pull out the crochet chain to expose live stitches.

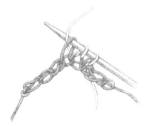

Long-Tail (Continental) Cast-On

Leaving a long tail (about ½" [1.3 cm] for each stitch to be cast on), make a slipknot and place on right needle. Place thumb and index finger of your left hand between the yarn ends so that working yarn is around your index finger and tail end is around your thumb and secure the yarn ends with your other fingers. Hold your palm upwards, making a V of yarn (Figure 1). *Bring needle up through loop on thumb (Figure 2), catch first strand around index finger, and go back down through loop on thumb (Figure 3). Drop loop off thumb and, placing thumb back in V configuration, tighten resulting stitch on needle (Figure 4). Repeat from * for the desired number of stitches.

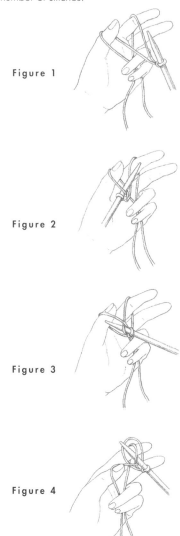

Figure 1

Figure 2

Figure 3

Figure 4

CRAFT YARN COUNCIL OF AMERICA

The Craft Yarn Council of America has set up guidelines to bring uniformity to yarn labels and published patterns. Yarns are classified according to the manufacturer's recommendations for gauge and needle size.

STANDARD YARN WEIGHT SYSTEM						
Yarn Weight Symbol and Category Name	**1** SUPER FINE	**2** FINE	**3** LIGHT	**4** MEDIUM	**5** BULKY	**6** SUPER BULKY
Type of Yarns in Category	Sock, Fingering, Baby	Sport, Baby	DK, Light Worsted	Worsted, Afghan, Aran	Chunky, Craft, Rug	Bulky, Roving
*Knitted Gauge Range in Stockinette Stitch to 4" (10 cm)	27–32 sts	23–26 sts	21–24 sts	16–20 sts	12–15 sts	6–11 sts
Recommended Needle in Metric Size Range	2.25–3.25 mm	3.25–3.75 mm	3.75–4.5 mm	4.5–5.5 mm	5.5–8 mm	8 mm and larger
Recommended Needle in U.S. Size Range	1–3	3–5	5–7	7–9	9–11	11 and larger
*Guidelines Only: The above reflect the most commonly used gauges and needles for specific yarn categories.						

CROCHET

Single Crochet (sc)

*Insert hook into the second chain from the hook (or the next stitch), yarn over hook and draw through a loop, yarn over hook (Figure 1), and draw it through both loops on hook (Figure 2). Repeat from * for the desired number of stitches.

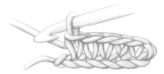

Figure 1   Figure 2

DECREASES

Ssk

Slip two stitches individually knitwise (Figure 1), insert left needle tip into the front of these two slipped stitches, and use the right needle to knit them together through their back loops (Figure 2).

Figure 1

Figure 2

Ssp

Holding yarn in front, slip two stitches individually knitwise (Figure 1), then slip these two stitches back onto left needle (they will be turned on the needle) and purl them together through their back loops (Figure 2).

Figure 1

Figure 2

EMBROIDERY

Chain Stitch

Bring threaded needle out from back to front at center of a knitted stitch. Form a short loop and insert needle back where it came out. Keeping the loop under the needle, bring needle back out in center of next stitch to the right.

Crochet Chain Stitch

Holding the yarn under the background, insert crochet hook through the center of a knitted stitch, pull up a loop, * insert hook into the center of the next stitch to the right, pull up a second loop through the first loop on the hook. Repeat from * as desired.

Stem Stitch

Bring threaded needle out of knitted background from back to front at the center of a knitted stitch. *Insert the needle into the upper right edge of the next stitch to the right, then out again at the center of the stitch below. Repeat from * as desired.

GRAFTING

Kitchener Stitch

Arrange stitches on two needles so that there is the same number of stitches on each needle. Hold the needles parallel to each other with right sides of the knitting facing up. Allowing about ½" (1.3 cm) per stitch to be grafted, thread matching yarn on a tapestry needle. Work from right to left as follows:

Step 1. Bring tapestry needle through the first stitch on the front needle as if to purl and leave the stitch on the needle (Figure 1).

Step 2. Bring tapestry needle through the first stitch on the back needle as if to knit and leave that stitch on the needle (Figure 2).

Step 3. Bring tapestry needle through the first front stitch as if to knit and slip this stitch off the needle, then bring seaming needle through the next front stitch as if to purl and leave this stitch on the needle (Figure 3).

Step 4. Bring tapestry needle through the first back stitch as if to purl and slip this stitch off the needle, then bring tapestry needle through the next back stitch as if to knit and leave this stitch on the needle (Figure 4).

Repeat Steps 3 and 4 until no stitches remain on the needles, adjusting the tension to match the rest of the knitting as you go.

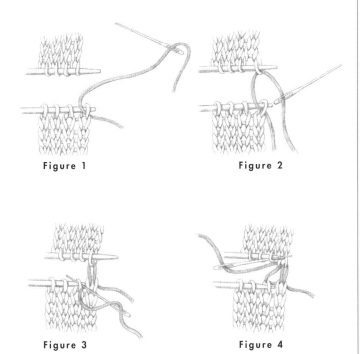

Figure 1   Figure 2

Figure 3   Figure 4

INCREASES

K1f&b

Knit into a stitch but leave it on the left needle (Figure 1), then knit through the back loop of the same stitch (Figure 2) and slip the original and new stitch off the needle (Figure 3).

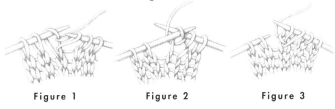

Figure 1   Figure 2   Figure 3

P1f&b

Purl into a stitch but leave it on the left needle (Figure 1), then purl through the back loop of the same stitch (Figure 2) and slip the original and new stitch off the needle.

Figure 1   Figure 2

KNIT-CORD

Using two double-pointed needles, cast on the desired number of stitches (usually 3 to 4). *Without turning the needle, slide stitches to other end of needle, pull the yarn around the back, and knit the stitches as usual. Repeat from * for desired length.

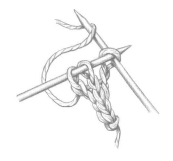

SEAMS

Invisible Horizontal Seam

Working with the bound-off edges opposite each other, right sides of the knitting facing you, and working into the stitches just below the bound-off edges, bring threaded tapestry needle out at the center of the first stitch (i.e., go under half of the first stitch) on one side of the seam, then bring needle in and out under the first whole stitch on the other side (Figure 1). *Bring needle into the center of the same stitch it came out of before, then out in the center of the adjacent stitch (Figure 2). Bring needle in and out under the next whole stitch on the other side (Figure 3). Repeat from *, ending with a half-stitch on the first side.

Invisible Vertical to Horizontal Seam

With yarn threaded on a tapestry needle, pick up one bar between the first two stitches along the vertical edge (Figure 1), then pick up one complete stitch along the horizontal edge (Figure 2). *Pick up the next one or two bars on the first piece, then the next whole stitch on the other piece (Figure 3). Repeat from *, ending by picking up one bar on the vertical edge.

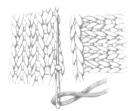

Figure 1

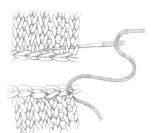

Figure 1

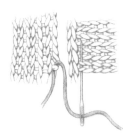

Figure 2

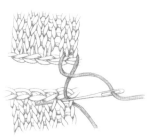

Figure 2

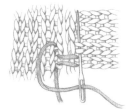

Figure 3

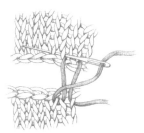

Figure 3

Mattress Stitch

Place the pieces to be seamed on a table, right sides facing up. Begin at the lower edge and work upward as follows for your stitch pattern:

Stockinette Stitch with One-Stitch Seam Allowance: *Insert threaded needle under one bar between the two edge stitches on one piece (Figure 1), then under the corresponding bar plus the bar above it on the other piece (Figure 2). *Pick up the next two bars on the first piece, then the next two bars on the other (Figure 3). Repeat from *, ending by picking up the last bar or pair of bars on the first piece.

Figure 1

Figure 2

Figure 3

Stockinette Stitch with Half-Stitch Seam Allowance: To reduce bulk in the mattress stitch seam, work as for the one-stitch seam allowance but pick up the bars in the center of the edge stitches instead of between the last two stitches.

Garter Stitch: Insert threaded needle under the lower horizontal bar between the two edge stitches on one piece (Figure 1), then the upper horizontal bar from the stitch next to the edge stitch on the same row of the other piece (Figure 2).

Figure 1

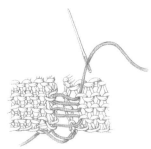

Figure 2

SEAMS (con't)

Slip-Stitch Crochet Seam

With right sides together and working one stitch at a time, *insert crochet hook through both thicknesses into the stitch just below the bound-off edge (or one stitch in from the selvedge edge), grab a loop of yarn (Figure 1), and draw this loop through both thicknesses, then through the loop on the hook (Figure 2). Repeat from *, keeping even tension on the crochet stitches.

Figure 1 Figure 2

Whipstitch

Hold pieces to be seamed together so that the edges to be seamed are even with each other. With yarn threaded on a tapestry needle, *insert needle through both layers from back to front, then bring needle to back. Repeat from *, keeping even tension on the seaming yarn.

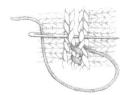

SHORT-ROWS

Work to turning point, slip next stitch purlwise, bring the yarn to the front (Figure 1), then slip the same stitch back to the left needle (Figure 2), turn the work around and bring the yarn in position for the next stitch, wrapping the slipped stitch with working yarn as you do so. When you come to a wrapped stitch on a subsequent row, hide the wrap by working it together with the wrapped stitch as follows: Insert right needle tip under the wrap (from the front if wrapped stitch is a knit stitch; from the back if wrapped stitch is a purl stitch; Figure 3), then into the stitch on the needle, and work the stitch and its wrap together as a single stitch.

Figure 1

Figure 2

Figure 3

SOURCES for SUPPLIES

Berroco Inc.
PO Box 367
14 Elmdale Rd.
Uxbridge, MA 01569
www.berroco.com
In Canada: S. R. Kertzer Ltd.
  Cotton Twist
  Glace
  Softwist

Blue Sky Alpacas Inc.
PO Box 88
Cedar, MN 55011
www.blueskyalpacas.com
  Dyed Cotton

Brown Sheep Company
100662 Cty. Rd. 16
Mitchell, NE 69357
www.brownsheep.com
  Lamb's Pride Super Wash
  Worsted

Cascade Yarns
PO Box 58168
1224 Andover Park East
Tukwila, WA 98188
www.cascadeyarns.com
  Sierra

Classic Elite Yarns
122 Western Ave.
Lowell, MA 01851
www.classiceliteyarns.com
  Fame
  Provence

Dale of Norway
N16 W23390 Stone Ridge
Dr., Ste. A
Waukesha, WI 53188
www.dale.no
  Tiur

Diamond Yarn
9697 St. Laurent, Ste. 101
Montreal, QC
Canada H3L 2N1
and
115 Martin Ross, Unit 3
Toronto, ON
Canada M3J 2L9
www.diamondyarn.com

Fiesta Yarns
4583 Corrales Rd.
Corrales, NM 87048
www.fiestayarns.com
  Meteor

JCA Inc./Reynolds
35 Scales Ln.
Townsend, MA 01469
www.jcacrafts.com
  Mandalay

S. R. Kertzer Ltd.
50 Trowers Rd.
Woodbridge, ON
Canada L4L 7K6
www.kertzer.com

**Knitting Fever Inc./
Debbie Bliss**
35 Debevoise Ave.
Roosevelt, NY 11575
www.knittingfever.com
In Canada: Diamond Yarn
  Debbie Bliss Pure Silk

Louet North America
808 Commerce Park Dr.
Ogdensburg, NY 13669
www.louet.com
In Canada:
RR #4
Prescott, ON K0E 1T0
  Euroflax Originals

CNS Yarns/Mission Falls
100 Walnut, Door 4
Champlain, NY 12919
www.missionfalls.com
In Canada:
1050 8th St.
Grand-Mère, QC G9T 4L4
  Mission Falls 1824 Cotton

Plymouth Yarn Co.
PO Box 28
Bristol, PA 19007
www.plymouthyarn.com
  Fantasy Naturale
  Linen Isle
  Royal Bamboo

BIBLIOGRAPHY

Barton, Jane, and Mary Kellogg Rice. *Shibori, The Inventive Art of Japanese Shaped Resist Dyeing*. Tokyo, New York, and San Francisco: Kodansha International Ltd, 1983.

Dalby, Liza Crihfield. *Kimono, Fashioning Culture*. Seattle and London: University of Washington Press, 1993.

Domyo, Mihoko, et al. *Masterpieces of Japanese Dress from the Bunka Gakuen Costume Museum*. Tokyo: Bunka Gakuen Costume Museum, 2000.

Hayao, Ishimura, and Maruyama Nobuhiko. *Robes of Elegance*. Raleigh, North Carolina: North Carolina Museum of Art, 1988.

Gonick, Gloria Granz. *Matsuri, Japanese Festival Arts*. Los Angeles: UCLA Fowler Museum of Cultural History, 2002.

Munsterberg, Hugo. *The Japanese Kimono*. Oxford, New York, Hong Kong: Oxford University Press, 1996.

Rathbun, William Jay, editor. *Beyond the Tanabata Bridge, Traditional Japanese Textiles*. Thames and Hudson in association with the Seattle Art Museum, 1993.

Stevens, Rebecca A. T., and Yoshiko Iwamoto Wada, editors. *The Kimono Inspiration*. San Francisco: Pomegranate Artbooks. Washington, D. C.: The Textile Museum, 1996.